T0361299

Cambridge Elements ≡

Elements in the Philosophy of Religion
edited by
Yujin Nagasawa
University of Birmingham

GOD AND TIME

Natalja Deng
Yonsei University, Seoul

CAMBRIDGE
UNIVERSITY PRESS

University Printing House, Cambridge CB2 8BS, United Kingdom

One Liberty Plaza, 20th Floor, New York, NY 10006, USA

477 Williamstown Road, Port Melbourne, VIC 3207, Australia

314–321, 3rd Floor, Plot 3, Splendor Forum, Jasola District Centre,
New Delhi – 110025, India

79 Anson Road, #06–04/06, Singapore 079906

Cambridge University Press is part of the University of Cambridge.

It furthers the University's mission by disseminating knowledge in the pursuit of
education, learning, and research at the highest international levels of excellence.

www.cambridge.org
Information on this title: www.cambridge.org/9781108455954
DOI: 10.1017/9781108653176

© Natalja Deng 2019

First published 2019

A catalogue record for this publication is available from the British Library.

ISBN 978-1-108-45595-4 Paperback
ISSN 2399-5165 (online)
ISSN 2515-9763 (print)

God and Time

Elements in the Philosophy of Religion

DOI: 10.1017/9781108653176
First published online: December 2018

Natalja Deng
Yonsei University, Seoul

Abstract: The God of Western religion is said to be eternal. But what does that mean? Is God somehow beyond time, living a life that does not involve one thing after another? Or is God's relationship to time much more like ours, so that God's eternality just consists in there being no time at which God does not exist? Even for nonbelievers, these issues have interesting implications for the relation between historical and scientific findings on the one hand, and religion on the other. This Element introduces the reader to the requisite metaphysical background, and then examines reasons for and against thinking of God as timeless.

Keywords: God, time, eternity, divine timelessness, divine temporality

ISBNs: 9781108455954 (PB), 9781108653176 (OC)
ISSNs: 2399–5165 (online), 2515–9763 (print)

Contents

1 Introduction

What does a person who is religious in the Western sense of the word, who believes in the traditional doctrines of a Western religion, believe? What is the content of their worldview? Of course, the answer varies for different religions – Judaism, Christianity, or Islam – and also for different denominations within those religions, but there will be some common themes. One such theme is the idea that God is personal, so that it is possible for human persons to have a relationship with God. Indeed, in many religious traditions, the quality of a person's relationship with God is a matter of great importance. It directly affects the flourishing, or otherwise, of every aspect of a human being's life. Another recurring theme is the idea that God is the creator of the universe.

This is an intriguing combination of ideas. What would a divine person who is the creator of the universe, and with whom many believers strive to cultivate a good relationship, be like? After all, God cannot be a physical being the way that human persons are. One way to narrow the investigation down a bit is to focus on God's relationship to time. Time is a ubiquitous aspect of our lives. After all, we are physical beings, whose lives are made up of events in time. We act in time, we age in time, and we try to show up to meetings on time. It is hard to think of a single aspect of our lives that is not deeply affected by the fact that we are temporal beings, whose life spans are temporally limited. God is not like that. True, according to believers, God is a person who often acts in time, who responds to petitionary prayers, and who affects world history. According to some traditions, God even has emotional reactions to things that happen in time. But God is also radically removed, and radically different, from us, and God's relationship to time is likely to reflect this. God is the creator of the universe, and the universe includes space and time. Does that mean God created space and time? And if so, does that in turn mean that God is somehow outside of time? And if God is outside of time, then how can God be (in some sense) present in our lives?

These questions, like many others in philosophy of religion, are of potential interest to both the believer and the nonbeliever. For the believer, they can be of existential significance. After all, they are, for the believer, about getting to know and trying to understand better the divine person with whom they take themselves to be in a relationship. Of course, there is no reason to expect to be able to fully understand the nature of God. But some questions about God's nature make a difference in how one feels able to relate to that divine being. Is God in the room with me now? Is God simultaneously in all other rooms? Does God know what it is like to anticipate, to wait, to change, or to think about the past? In what ways do we human beings experience these things differently?

Does God know what I'm going through right at this moment? Has God always known?

To the nonbeliever, questions about God and time may matter for different reasons. God's relation to time is a defining element of any conception of God, one that has repercussions throughout one's theology and wider worldview. Time is a central aspect of the natural world. How one conceives of God's relation to aspects of the natural world directly affects whether and to what extent there can be (dis)confirmation of God's existence on the basis of historical or empirical findings. Do science and religion have any bearing on one another, and if so, are they in tension? Do the historical and scientific bodies of evidence support a favorable or an unfavorable stance on whether God exists? One need not be undecided on these questions in order to be interested in how best to defend one's answers to them. Entering into reasoned dialogue about religion, science, and history can require pursuing topics that might previously have seemed of interest only to the believer. God's relation to time is one of these topics.

Supposing one has decided to consider the question of God's relationship to time, how can one hope to make progress with it? What methodology can be fruitfully employed here? There is a lot to be said about this, because many different disciplines are involved to some degree, including philosophy of religion, philosophy of time, and philosophical theology. Moreover, there are various approaches to each of these. Here it will suffice to say a bit about the methodology employed in this Element. The aim of the Element is to introduce the reader to the current state of art of philosophical thinking about God and time, without presupposing much more than a basic curiosity about the topic. So the focus is on the contemporary philosophical discussion. Of course, there is a long and fascinating history of thought about the topic. And it is not always useful or even possible to neatly separate that history from the ways philosophers and theologians are approaching the topic nowadays. The approach taken here will be to look at the history through contemporary lenses, whenever this is helpful for understanding or evaluating current thinking about the topic. Naturally, there has to be a certain selection of views. This is done largely on the basis of how prominent a role these views have played in the philosophical literature, but also with a view to presenting a balanced and wide-ranging introduction to the philosophical landscape.

So, what are philosophy of religion, philosophy of time, and philosophical theology, and what can each of these contribute? Philosophy of religion, unsurprisingly, is the part of philosophy that asks philosophical questions about religion. That includes, among other things, the evaluation of a variety of arguments for and against the existence of God, or for and against the (in) coherence of various religious ideas. The present topic is a part of philosophy of religion. Philosophy of time is the part of philosophy concerned with the nature of time, our experience of time, and the relation between the two. Philosophy of time is a field to which many different scientific disciplines, including both physics and cognitive science, are relevant in different ways; and it is increasingly being conducted in a way that draws these fields together. However, there is also a part of the philosophy of time – called the metaphysics of time – that is a bit more traditional. Since it is this part of the philosophy of time that has played the greatest role in the God and time discussion to date, much of the next section is devoted to it. Briefly, in metaphysics one asks questions about the most general and/or most basic features of reality. Therefore, in the metaphysics of time, one asks questions about the most general and/or most basic features of *temporal* reality. What is the nature of time? How much like space is it? Does it pass or flow – that is, does it have a dynamic aspect that space lacks? If so, what does this passing consist in? These questions are dealt with in the metaphysics of time. Finally, by "philosophical theology" I mean an approach to theological questions that aims for conceptual clarity and that values thinking about the merits of arguments for and against claims.

As our topic is the God of Western religion, there are methodological constraints arising from relevant passages in Western Scripture.[1] Partly for historical reasons, much of the contemporary discussion is focused on the Judeo-Christian, especially the Christian, tradition. The Bible contains many relevant passages (Leftow 2005). For example, there are passages telling us that God's "years have no end" (Ps. 102:27, all quotations are from the New Revised Standard Version) and that God exists "from everlasting to everlasting" (Pss. 90:2, 103:17). God says, "let there be lights in the dome of the sky to separate the day from the night, and let them be for signs and for seasons and for days and years" (Gen. 1:14), and "I am the first and I am the last" (Isa. 44:6). Moreover, we are told that God promised us eternal life "before the ages began" (Titus 1:2), and that "He himself is before all things" (Col. 1:17). Making sense of these passages requires philosophical work.

There are two key terms that will reoccur throughout the Element. First, "theism" refers to the view that there is a personal God who is omniscient, omnipotent, and omnibenevolent, who created the world, and who is still actively involved in the world. This is intended to capture a core view at the heart of all three Western religions (Judaism, Islam, Christianity). The topic of

---

[1] The rest of this section, as well as parts of Sections 3 and 4, contain developments of many ideas that first appeared in the SEP article "Eternity in Christian Thought" (Deng 2018b).

this Element is the relation between time and the God of Western theism. However, as mentioned, much of the contemporary discussion focuses on the Judeo-Christian, especially the Christian, tradition. (But note that we will not discuss specific Christian doctrines such as the doctrine of the Trinity or the Incarnation.)

The second key term is "eternity" (and "God's eternality"). In philosophical discussions about God and time, the term "eternity" has been used in different ways. On one usage, which will be followed here, "eternity" stands for the relationship to time that God has, whatever it is. When used in that way, the term is neutral between different ways of spelling out what God's relationship to time is. Theists agree that God is eternal; the task is to formulate and assess conceptions of what this eternality might amount to.

Broadly speaking, there have been two rival views of God's eternality. These will be explained in much more detail in the coming sections; the following is just intended to provide the reader with a rough overview. In the first of the two views, God is timeless or outside of time (divine timelessness). In the second, God is not outside of time, but rather in time (divine temporality). Sometimes the term "eternity" is used to denote divine timelessness, but we will here use it as neutral between the timeless and temporal views. The term "everlasting" (or "sempiternal") on the other hand, is strongly associated with the temporal view. On the temporal view, God is in time and exists at every time; there is no time at which God does not exist.

This twofold opposition is a good rough guide to the landscape. However, here is the first complication. So far, I've talked as if there are two broad rival positions on a single issue, namely of how God relates to time. But there are actually at least two orthogonal issues regarding God's relationship to time: (1) whether God is located in our spacetime – the spacetime investigated by modern physics; and (2) whether God is timeless or temporal, in the sense of either having or not having a life that is "marked by temporal succession." God could be timeless in the sense of having a life that is not "marked by temporal succession" while being located at every spacetime point. Conversely, God could be temporal in the sense of having a life "marked by temporal succession" while not being located in physical spacetime at all (Rea and Murray 2008, ch. 2).

At first glance, this distinction can seem somewhat mysterious: If the issue is not being located in our physical spacetime, then what is it? What can the second issue be? What can it mean to say that an entity is temporal if that does not commit one to a view on whether that entity is located in spacetime? Aren't times somehow to be understood in terms of spacetime, ultimately?

The answer is that the first question is about whether God is located in spacetime (and relatedly, whether God exists in time, i.e., at times); while the second is about (for want of a better phrase) the nature of God's experience. Whether or not a subject experiences succession, and more generally, what the (a)temporal features of its experience are, is an issue distinct from whether or not that subject is located in spacetime. It is true that normally there are connections between these issues. For us, for example, these facts are related. It is partly because we are located in spacetime that we experience one thing after the other, and there are interesting questions about the details of this connection. But the issues are conceptually distinct. And the same distinction can in principle be made regarding God.

These two issues are not always separated in some of the existing literature. The result is that divine timelessness views and divine temporality views often involve claims both about whether God is located in time/spacetime and about (a)temporal features of God's experience. Specifically, divine timelessness views may involve both the claim that God is not located in time/spacetime, and the claim that God does not experience succession. Similarly, divine temporality views may involve both the claim that God is in time/spacetime and that God experiences succession.

One final point of methodology may already have occurred to the reader. Should theological commitments be allowed to determine one's views about the metaphysics, or even the physics of time? A salient alternative would be to do the opposite, for example by taking as one's starting point the metaphysical view of time suggested by our best physical theories and then drawing out any theological implications. A third approach might involve giving equal weight to both poles and seeking to come to a coherent and adequate conception of both time and God as part of the same endeavor. There probably exist a variety of stances on this question within both philosophy and theology. (For explicit reflection on related methodological questions see, e.g., Rea and Murray 2008, 47; Mullins 2016, ch. 1.)

Let us start by taking a closer look at the metaphysics of time and persistence. Both of these form part of the metaphysical background that we will draw on in later sections.

2 Time and Persistence

To understand God's relationship to time, one has to have an idea of what time is like, and of how things exist in time. The metaphysics of time provides us with some options for how to think about what temporal reality might be like. In later sections, we will see that metaphysical distinctions in the philosophy of time have often been taken to have a more direct impact on the God and time discussion than they really have. But this still means it is important to start out with a clear understanding of those metaphysical distinctions. Similarly, the metaphysics of persistence provides us with some options for how to think of the relation between time and things in time. We will consider these in turn, going into just enough detail as needed to provide the reader with the necessary metaphysical background.[2]

The contemporary landscape in the metaphysics of time is characterized by a debate between A-theorists and B-theorists. Of the A-theory there are many different versions, while the B-theory is more uniform. Roughly speaking, these two theories are divided over the question of whether time really passes (or flows) – whether it has a dynamic aspect that space lacks. A-theorists think it does, while B-theorists think it does not. To see what is involved in this, consider a few different versions of the A-theory (the following is by no means an exhaustive survey). Presentists think that only the present exists, and that time's passing consists in new times' coming into and other times' going out of existence. Growing block theorists think that the past and present both exist, but the future does not. According to them, time's passing consists in new times' coming into existence. Reality is an ever growing block whose edge is the present time. Yet another version of the A-theory, the moving spotlight view, says that all times exist (this is known as eternalism), but that only one of them is ever absolutely present. By this, moving spotlighters mean that only one time ever is present in a sense that goes beyond the merely relative sense, in which every time is present relative to itself. Times gain and shed absolute presentness, and that is what time's passing consists in. There are lots of other versions of the A-theory. (Moreover, it should be noted that this survey is simplified in other ways; for example, not everyone agrees that all versions of presentism are in fact versions of the A-theory [Tallant 2012].)

B-theorists also are eternalists – they too think that all times exist. However, they disagree with moving spotlighters on the key question of whether any one time is ever present in an absolute sense. B-theorists deny this. According to them, each time is present relative to itself, and that is all. This reflects their commitment to treating time as similar to space in important respects. All spatial locations exist, and each of them is "here" relative to itself; but none of them is here in an absolute sense. It is the same with time, according to B-theorists. More generally, no time is metaphysically privileged in any way. This rules out ontological privilege, such as being the only or the latest time that

---

[2] Some of the ideas covered in the first half of this section also appear in "Time, metaphysics of" (Deng, forthcoming in the REP).

exists, as well as other metaphysical privileges, such as being absolutely present. All times are metaphysically on a par.

I said that A-theorists and B-theorists differ over whether time passes. More carefully, we might say (following Skow 2015, 2) that they differ over whether time passes, in a metaphysically robust sense: they differ over whether times gain and shed some metaphysical privilege in turn. That is, the debate is about time's passing in a very specific, somewhat technical sense. How this technical sense relates to what ordinary people have in mind when they talk about time's passing is to some extent an open (empirical) question. Certainly B-theorists need not disagree with one who says, for example, "A lot of time has passed since the dawn of the Internet," or "Time is passing: it is now 8 PM, and it was 7.35 PM a little while ago." It is just that for the B-theorist, what this comes to is, in the first case, that there is a long temporal interval between the dawn of the Internet and the speaker's utterance, and in the second case, that there is a short temporal interval between 7.35 PM and the speaker's utterance. What the B-theorist denies is that there is more to time's passing than this – more than there being different times that succeed one another, and between which there lie temporal intervals of various lengths. What the B-theorist denies is that time passes in a metaphysically robust sense in which temporal passage would involve one time's gaining and shedding metaphysical privilege, like being absolutely present, or being the only time that exists, or being the latest time that exists. Robust temporal passage is also sometimes referred to as "temporal becoming" or "flow."

The A- and the B-theories are also sometimes known as the dynamic and the static theories of time, or as the tensed and the tenseless theories of time, respectively. The latter labels are linguistic in origin, and they reflect a long-standing interest by philosophers of time in how temporal language works. The B-theory, or tenseless theory, can be thought of as the combination of eternalism with the claim that there is a completely tenseless description of temporal reality. A tenseless description of temporal reality is one that stays accurate over time. It mentions only tenseless facts concerning when events happen and how they are temporally related to one another. An example of a tenseless fact is that my writing this sentence occurs (tenselessly) on a Monday. The B-theorist thinks there is a complete description of temporal reality that is entirely tenseless. Another interesting question is how one should understand the notion of "completeness" in play here; most likely it is best understood by reference to such notions as which descriptions are more fundamental than others, or which notions carve nature at its joints. So the B-theory can also be taken to be the combination of eternalism with the claim that there is a tenseless description of reality that is more fundamental than any tensed description.

A-theorists deny this. For them, some tensed description of temporal reality will be more fundamental than any tenseless one. A tensed description of temporal reality is a description that mentions tensed facts, such as that it is Monday today. These facts change, so the description does not stay accurate over time. In fact, their changing is what the robust passage of time amounts to. First it is a tensed fact that it is Monday, then it is a tensed fact that it is Tuesday and that it was Monday one day ago. But according to the A-theorist, if one leaves out the tensed fact that it is Monday, then one leaves out something essential, and the resulting description of temporal reality will be radically incomplete.

The B-theorists thinks of time as being much like space in this respect. Not many people would think that in a complete description of spatial reality, one has to include such ("spatially tensed") facts as that this room is well air conditioned, or that it is hilly around here. Rather, one only has to include such ("spatially tenseless") facts as which objects are located where at which spatial locations, and how those objects and spatial locations are spatially related to one another. The reason the A-theorist disagrees is connected to their conviction that time has a dynamic aspect that space lacks, that time passes in a metaphysically robust sense. In John Norton's words, "Time passes. Nothing fancy is meant by that. It is just the mundane fact known to us all that future events will become present and then drift off into the past" (Norton 2010, 24). If one takes this metaphysical statement seriously, one needs to posit fundamental tensed facts: first the facts that t_1 is present, t_0 was, and t_2 will be, then the tensed facts that t_2 is present, t_1 was, and t_3 will be, and so on.

In a way, something like the A- versus B-distinction goes back to Heraclitus and Parmenides, and many historical thinkers can be read as implicitly or explicitly defending one of these two theories. But the particular form of the contemporary debate has its origin in the work of the British idealist J. M. E. McTaggart. McTaggart recognized that there are two different ways of lining up the events of world history: in an A-series, or in a B-series (McTaggart 1908). The A-series runs from the past through the present and into the future, while the B-series runs from earlier to later. The difference between these two ways of thinking becomes clear if one notices that while, for example, it is always true to say that World War I happened before World War II, it is not now true to say that World War II is in the future. McTaggart recognized that in ordinary life, we need both of these ways of thinking of time. But he posed the further question of which of these series is more fundamental than the other. And according to McTaggart, the answer is that the A-series is more fundamental.

Ultimately, McTaggart argued for the conclusion that time is not real. He did this in several steps. First, he argued for the claim that there is time only if there can be change. Then he argued that there can be change only if events are part of an A-series, so that they have what he called A-properties, such as pastness, presentness, or futurity. The reason McTaggart gives for this is that B-properties – such as being simultaneous with or being earlier than – are properties that events never gain or shed. Once you have a B-property, you keep it. From this McTaggart inferred that in order for there to be the possibility of change, the A-series has to be real. So, in order for time to exist, the A-series has to be real. However, and this is the final part of his argument, the A-series is contradictory, and therefore it is not real. Why is it contradictory, according to McTaggart? There are many different reconstructions of this step, and opinions in the philosophy of time have been sharply divided over the question of whether there is anything right about this step. But according to McTaggart, the reason the A-series is contradictory is that if an event has any A-property, then it has all of them – after all, the present is something that *moves on*. If any event is ever (absolutely) present, then it is also (absolutely) past and (absolutely) future. But these are incompatible properties. So no event can have them all. Therefore, no event has any A-property.

McTaggart anticipates the objection that each event only ever has one of these A-properties at a time. His reply is that the objection relies on what had to be shown: the reply involves the notion of an event's having a property *at a time*, when the whole task was to show how temporality emerges from an A-series. He says that by "at a time," the objector must mean that a present event was future and will be past, where that in turn means that it is future at a past time and past at a future time. But that means that in order to explain how an event can have A-properties, the objector has to rely on its having further (higher-order) A-properties. In order to show that there is nothing contradictory about the A-series in the first place, the objector has to assume that there are further (non-contradictory) A-series, which means the objector has not come to grips with the threat of contradiction.

As mentioned, opinions divide sharply over the merits of this argument. There are those who think it contains an important insight (e.g., Dummett 1960; Horwich 1987; Mellor 1998; Fine 2006) and those who think it is a glorified mistake (e.g., Broad 1938, 316; Sider 2001; Zimmerman 2005). Those in the latter group may feel forced to conclude that McTaggart's decision not to put forward a similar argument about space was a mere oversight. Those in the former group are likely to think that on the contrary, McTaggart had good reason to say what he said about time in particular (cf. Deng 2013a).

The overall shape of the A versus B dialectic is that the A-theory is often seen as capturing the way we ordinarily think about and experience time, while the B-theory is seen as being closer to the results of modern physics. Both of these aspects of the A versus B debate play a role in the discussion about God and time. So let us look at each of them, starting with the relation between physics and the A-theory.

The A-theory faces a formidable challenge arising from Einstein's theory of relativity. Recall that the A-theory makes central use of the idea that the present is metaphysically privileged in some way. A reason one might worry about this idea has to do with the idea of "metaphysical privilege." But another, physics-based reason to worry about it is that in relativity theory, it is not clear what can count as "the present."

Most likely, what we mean by "the present" is something like reality as it is everywhere right now, i.e., a global now. But it is an important lesson of relativity theory that there is no such thing as a global now. Which spatially distant events are simultaneous with a given event is something that varies with one's state of motion (something that is different in different frames of reference). Distant simultaneity no longer exists. As a result, the idea of a global now that has metaphysical significance becomes hard to sustain.

There have been a number of different reactions to this problem. Some amount to either a modification or an augmentation of special relativity. (The above problem is one that arises in Einstein's special theory of relativity; but the situation is not much helped by moving to the general theory.) In the "neo-Lorentzian interpretation" of special relativity, an example of the modification strategy, one maintains that simultaneity is absolute, rather than relative to a frame of reference (e.g., Tooley 1997; Craig 2001). There is a privileged frame of reference, namely the one at rest with respect to absolute space, and real simultaneity is simultaneity in this privileged frame of reference. However, which frame this is, is in principle undetectable by any empirical means. The relativistic effects of length contraction and time dilation conspire to hide the frame from us. That matter exhibits these effects – that it is effectively governed by laws that are Lorentz invariant – is an unexplained fact. That fact is not explainable in terms of the symmetries of spacetime.

A different response to the challenge seeks to augment special relativity, in the following sense. Suppose that, unlike on the neo-Lorentzian interpretation, one acknowledges that the background spacetime of special relativity is Minkowski spacetime. One can still maintain that the contents of spacetime privilege one way of "slicing up" (foliating) spacetime into slices of simultaneous events (e.g., Zimmerman 2011, 215). The distribution of matter happens to privilege one such foliation, and one frame of reference.

A much less radical response seeks to alleviate the tension through modification on the side of the metaphysics, rather than the physics. In particular, one might try to remove the need for a global now from various versions of the A-theory. Earman 2008 does this for the growing block view, Skow 2009 for the moving spotlight view (see Pooley 2013 for further discussion). Finally, an A-theorist might also accept that, within the confines of relativity theory, there is not much hope for the A-theory, but point out that relativity theory is not the last word. Traditionally, certain interpretations of non-relativistic quantum mechanics, such as Bohmian mechanics and collapse theories, have been a source of hope for A-theorists. Moreover, at the frontiers of physics, there are some approaches to quantum gravity (the prospective physical theory that combines quantum theory with general relativity) that have been presented as hospitable to an A-theoretic metaphysics. In particular, the causal set theory approach may be suggestive of something like the growing block view (e.g., Wüthrich and Callender 2017; Earman 2008).

While the A-theory has the disadvantage that modern physics is not very hospitable to it, the B-theory arguably has the disadvantage of clashing with the view of time suggested by ordinary temporal experience. But is there really a clash, and how is that clash best expressed? And if there is a clash, (how) can B-theorists explain why we experience time in misleading ways?

There are many different aspects to the problem. One way to approach it is to start with a distinction between two meanings of the term "temporal experience." Consider the following quote by Robin Le Poidevin:

> We are indirectly aware of the passage of time when we reflect on our memories, which present the world as it was, and so a contrast with how things are now. But much more immediate than this is seeing the second hand move around the clock, or hearing a succession of notes in a piece of music, or feeling a raindrop run down your neck. There is nothing inferential, it seems, about the perception of change and motion: it is simply given in experience. (Le Poidevin 2007, 87)

From this we can distill two senses of "temporal experience." The first is the direct one, where "temporal experience" refers to our perceptual experience of time. Admittedly, it can seem strange to think of time as something that is perceived. After all, time is not an object like a chair or a laptop, and we do not perceive time in the way we perceive those things. But still, we perceive, it seems, temporal features of the world. We perceive one thing following on from another, and things lasting for certain intervals. That is, we perceive succession and duration, for instance. These are temporal features of the world. Temporal experience in this first sense is something that happens on short time scales – that is non-inferential and immediate.

The second sense of "temporal experience" is broader. Presumably, Le Poidevin does not mean to draw the contrast merely by reference to whether memory is involved (since he himself thinks that memory is involved in temporal experience on short time scales too). Rather, what he has in mind is temporal experience over longer time scales than we can perceive. When seeing a second hand move around a clock, we are perceiving temporal features. But in reflecting on how the hour hand has moved, we are doing something different – or something more: not only do we perceive where the hour hand is now, but we compare that with where we remember the hour hand to have been. This is a more voluntary process, something that is different in quality from, and more indirect than, perceptual awareness.

One question that the discussion has focused on is whether temporal experience in the first, perceptual sense, involves the robust passage of time (i.e., the passage of time understood A-theoretically). A-theorists have long pointed to the nature of temporal experience on short time scales to support their view. And even many B-theorists have taken for granted that this is the right way to characterize perceptual temporal experience. To quote Le Poidevin once more: "We just *see* time passing in front us, in the movement of a second hand around a clock, or the falling of sand through an hourglass, or indeed any motion or change at all" (Le Poidevin 2007, 76).

The argument implicit here can be thought of as an inference to the best explanation (Baron et al. 2015). (1) We have experiences as of time (robustly) passing. (2) If we have experiences as of time (robustly) passing, then any reasonable explanation of this relies on the (robust) passage of time being an objective feature of reality. (3) Hence, the (robust) passage of time is an objective feature of reality. The "as of" is intended to signal that we are not assuming here that the experiences in question are veridical, i.e., we are not assuming that they represent temporal reality accurately. Following Baron et al., we can call B-theorists who reject (2) but accept (1) illusionists, and B-theorists who reject (1) veridicalists. Illusionists think that we have perceptual experiences as of time robustly passing, even though time does not robustly pass. Veridicalists think that we do not have perceptual experiences as of time robustly passing, and that time does not robustly pass.

Some illusionists have turned to cognitive science to try to explain away what they think of as the perceptual illusion of the robust passage of time. One example is Laurie Paul (Paul 2010). Paul suggests thinking the perception of change and motion in a B-theoretic universe as analogous to perceptual illusions of change and motion. The illusions she has in mind include flipbooks, as well as our perception of continuity rather than a series of still images in movies. But her central example is what in the philosophical literature has become known as the color phi phenomenon. Here, a subject is presented with a series of flashes of a differently colored dot on opposite sides of a screen (red dot top, green dot bottom, red dot top, etc.). If the flashes are timed and spaced appropriately, the subject can have an illusion as of a single dot moving back and forth continuously and changing its color abruptly, somewhere along the trajectory.

Paul's idea is that we should understand the veridical perception of motion and change in a B-theoretic world along similar lines. Consider a change in an object O, understood as the B-theorist thinks of it: O has property P at t_1, and a different, incompatible property Q at t_2. When we perceive these tenseless facts, our brain "fills in" information due to its limited powers of discrimination. So what we end up perceiving (or having perceptual experiences as of) are tensed facts, namely, first, the object's presently being P and then the object's presently being Q and having been P. Life as a whole, then, is a kind of film, on this view. Because of that, we are subject to a constant perceptual illusion of robust passage. But when we are undergoing a color phi experiment, or watching a film, then we are undergoing a second perceptual illusion, in addition to that of robust passage, namely that of change or motion. In both cases, the brain "responds to closely spaced inputs that have sufficient similarity (yet have qualitative contrasts of some sort) by accommodating and organizing the inputs," thereby creating a sense of "animated change," which is change that involves robust passage (Paul 2010, 22).

But there are some problems with this proposal. Interestingly, these problems are not entirely unrelated to problems with allusions to the B-theory in the context of divine timelessness (see Section 3). The B-theory, recall, says that all times exist and no time is metaphysically privileged in any way, so that at the fundamental level, there are only tenseless facts. It does not involve a claim about whether time is discrete or continuous. The tenseless facts it posits are not themselves in time, so that they are not themselves perceived for a while, like the static flashes in the color phi experiment (which are perceived for short durations, during which they do not change). Of course, the idea is that there is a fruitful analogy to be had here. But whether this analogy is fruitful depends on whether we can use the empirically well documented perceptual mechanism that is in play in perceptual illusions to shed light on the (alleged) illusion of robust passage. It is not clear how we can do that. The problem is that in order for the analogy to work, we have to pretend that there is, on the B-theory, discreteness, or rather "gappiness" of the kind found in the color phi phenomenon. But then what we will have explained is an illusion of continuity, of continuous motion and persistence. And if that was all that needed explaining, on the B-theory, then veridicalists were right, and there is no extra illusion of robust passage to be explained (Deng 2013b; Hoerl 2014ab).

All this is not to say that there are no interesting questions left about the B-theory and its relation to temporal experience, in both the narrow and the broad senses. There are a variety of stances on this issue (e.g., Grünbaum 1967; Butterfield 1984; Mellor 2001; Falk 2003; Skow 2015; Ismael 2011; Prosser 2016; Callender 2017; Baron et al. 2015; and Phillips 2017 contain further useful references). Some authors are also questioning the ability of A-theorists to account for the nature of temporal experience (Frischhut 2013; Dorato 2015; Prosser 2016), and the role that temporal experience can play in a metaphysical debate (Benovsky 2013). Finally, note that some authors connect the issue of the B-theory's relation to temporal experience with questions about the structure of temporal experience, and about how we perceive temporal extent at all (Tallant 2013; Dainton 2008; Phillips 2010). This is the part of the literature in which the term "specious present" is sometimes used.

Let us now move on from time to persistence.[3] There is generally thought to be a metaphysical issue about how things persist over time. The term "thing" is being used very widely here, to denote material objects. This includes, for example, tables, laptops, rivers, mountains, stars, galaxies, human beings, and other animals. The term "persistence" is used to denote the existence of things over time, or through time. How things manage to do this – what it is that their persistence consists in – is what needs to be settled in order to settle the issue of persistence.

There are three major metaphysical theories about what how things persist. The first is endurantism. This is the view that things persist by surviving from one time to the next, where this survival amounts to strict numerical identity. So in order to understand endurantism, one has to first understand the difference between qualitative and numerical identity. In ordinary life, we might say "those two jackets look identical," or "those two jackets are identical." What we mean by that is that the two look exactly alike. This is what is called qualitative identity. Objects a and b are qualitatively identical just in case they share all of the same qualities – color, shape, size, etc. What metaphysicians usually call identity is not qualitative identity, but numerical identity. This is what obtains when objects a and b really are one and the same object. That is, there are two names – "a" and "b" – and they both stand for the same object.

---

[3] What follows is loosely based on the exposition in Chapter 6 of Ney 2014.

This is numerical identity ("numerical" because it amounts to there being only one object here), or identity in the strict sense.

Again, endurantism is the view that things persist by surviving from one time to another, where this survival involves strict numerical identity. For example, suppose a coffee mug comes into existence at some time t_0 and then persists until t_3 (suppose it is smashed at t_3). The endurantist thinks that the mug persists over this interval because there is an object (the mug) at t_0 that is identical with an object (the mug) at t_1, and with the object (again, the mug) existing at t_2 and t_3 as well. This is one view to take of how the mug manages to exist over time. It is how an endurantist views the mug's persistence.

At this point, endurantism may sound obviously true. How else could things persist? But now consider a different view of persistence, perdurantism (also called the worm view). Perdurantism is the view that things persist over time by being spread out or extended over it. According to perdurantists, things persist by having not only spatial parts, but also temporal parts (or stages). So, material objects are temporally extended. They are four-dimensional, in the sense that they are spread out in time – the fourth dimension – just like they are spread out in the three spatial dimensions. Just as objects have different spatial parts, such as arms and legs, in different places, so objects have different temporal parts, such as earlier halves and later halves, a childhood part and an adulthood part, and so on. And that is how they persist through time. Just like you are currently managing to exist through space by having some spatial parts of yours near the floor and some others further away from the floor, so you persist through time by having some temporal parts of yours located at earlier times than others. That is perdurantism.

Consider the coffee mug again, this time viewed as the perdurantist views it. Recall that the coffee mug exists over the temporal interval from t_0 to t_3. So the coffee mug persists from t_0 to t_3. That much both sides agree on. But the perdurantist thinks that there is something that exists at t_0 that is not the mug, but only one temporal part (or stage) of the mug. Similarly, at t_1 there exists another temporal part of the mug, and so on. The part that exists at t_0 is not strictly speaking identical with the part at t_1. The temporal parts of the mug are no more numerically identical than the mug's left and right half, or your left and right arm. And the way the mug manages to exist over time is by having all these temporal parts located at those different times.

Perdurantism is partly motivated by the conviction that we should treat time the same way as space in our metaphysics. This it shares with eternalism (the view that all times exist), since we do not ordinarily deny reality to any spatial location – for example, Australia is just as real as the United Kingdom. Similarly, the B-theory also treats time as on a par with space in the sense that no time is metaphysically privileged, just like, as we would ordinarily think, no spatial location is metaphysically privileged. But it should be noted that there is no entailment from the B-theory to perdurantism, much less from eternalism to perdurantism.

How do endurantism and perdurantism differ? Suppose an endurantist described their view by emphasizing that in endurantism, things persist by existing at different times. That would not suffice to demarcate their view. After all, a perdurantist can agree: things persist by existing at different times, and the way things exist at different times is by having temporal parts that exist at each of those times. Or suppose the endurantist said that in endurantism, things persist by being the same object from one moment to the next.

That would not do either. The perdurantist agrees, because in perdurantism, the temporally extended mug is the same object from one moment to the next; it is just the mug's temporal parts that are not.

So, endurantists need to say more to distinguish their view from perdurantism. What they say is that in endurantism, the persisting thing is *wholly present* at each time at which it exists. The entire mug is there at t_0, and the entire mug is there at each of the other times. Of course this raises further questions about how best to understand the notion of being *wholly present*. But for our purposes, what matters is just that this is a common way to formulate endurantism. Endurantism is the view that things persist by being wholly present at each time they exist, where to be wholly present at a time is, roughly, to have all of one's parts exist at that time.

Endurantism is usually combined with three-dimensionalism. Three-dimensionalists deny that any objects have temporal parts in addition to spatial parts. Three-dimensionalism is so called because it sees objects as extended only in the three spatial dimensions, by having a height, a length, and a width. All of the material parts of an object are spatial parts. Three-dimensionalists do not deny that things persist, but they deny that they persist by having temporal parts. Perdurantists reject three-dimensionalism and accept instead four-dimensionalism. This is the view that at least some objects have temporal parts.[4] Perdurantists have to be four-dimensionalists, since they think objects persist by having temporal parts (and at least some objects do persist). But there are ways of being a four-dimensionalist without accepting perdurantism (more on this below).

Apart from the conviction that time is like space in many respects, perdurantism is also often motivated by appeal to various metaphysical puzzles,

---

[4] Sometimes, "four-dimensionalism" is used to denote instead perdurantism, or else the combination of perdurantism and the B-theory. That is not the usage followed here.

which it is said to help solve. A central such puzzle is the problem of temporary intrinsics proposed by David Lewis (Lewis 1986). Knowing about this problem will help us understand the third main position on persistence, apart from endurantism and perdurantism. To begin with, note that many of the properties that objects have over the course of their histories are intrinsic properties – properties that objects have just in virtue of how they are in themselves, not how they are in relation to other things. An example might be the size or shape of an object. An object that is spherical or that has a certain volume seems to have those properties just in virtue of how it is in itself. These are intrinsic properties of it. By contrast, being a father or an aunt or the tallest man alive are not intrinsic properties, because they are had in virtue of how things are in relation to other entities.

The problem of temporary intrinsics arises because objects gain and shed intrinsic properties. That is, many of the intrinsic properties objects have are properties they have only temporarily. For example, sometimes you are standing and thereby have a certain fairly straight shape, whereas at other times, you are sitting and thereby have a certain more bent shape. Suppose you're straight at time t_0 and bent at time t_1 (because you sit down). And suppose we think of your persistence in endurantist terms. Then we will think you are wholly present at both times, and the entity that exists at t_0 (you) is identical with the entity that exists at t_1 (you). So one and the same entity is both straight and bent, which are incompatible intrinsic properties. This is thought to be a problem for endurantism, because it is in conflict with the metaphysical principle known as Leibniz's Law (or the Indiscernibility of Identicals). Leibniz's Law says that necessarily, if a and b are identical, then they share all their properties. (This is not to be confused with the far more controversial Identity of Indiscernibles, which says that necessarily, if a and b are qualitative duplicates (qualitatively identical), then they are the same object (numerically identical).) If "Fido" and "Doggie" name the same dog, then Fido has no properties that Doggie lacks, and vice versa.

Lewis considers and rejects a number of ways the endurantist might try to solve the problem of temporary intrinsics. One is to accept presentism. The thought is roughly that in presentism we can avoid the contradiction, because nothing is ever bent and straight *at once*. At t_0 something *is* straight and *will be* bent, while at t_1 something *is* bent and *was* straight. A second endurantist response Lewis considers involves maintaining eternalism, but taking properties that may seem intrinsic at first sight (like shape) to be relational at root. Objects only have shapes in relation to times. You are never intrinsically bent (there is no such thing as being intrinsically bent), you just have the relational property of being-straight-at-t_0, and the relational property of being-bent-at-t_1.

As mentioned, Lewis rejects both of these endurantist responses to the problem. Perdurantism presents a different solution, or rather prevention, of the problem: nothing has incompatible properties, because your sitting down involves your having a temporal part that is straight, which exists at t_0, and your having a different temporal part that is bent, which exists at t_1. There is no conflict with Leibniz's Law. Shapes are intrinsic properties, but they are had by temporal parts of objects. In general, objects manage to change in their intrinsic properties, simply by having different temporal parts with different, incompatible intrinsic properties. This is no more puzzling than having different spatial parts with different, incompatible intrinsic properties, such as your left arm's being bent and your right arm's being straight.

But does not perdurantism then prevent us from saying that it is the persisting object itself that has the intrinsic properties in question? And is that not highly counterintuitive? In perdurantism, it seems to be something else that is bent and straight, not you. It is just your temporal parts that are bent or straight, not you yourself, the temporally extended worm with many temporal parts. At least that temporally extended worm that is you does not *directly* have these intrinsic properties.

In response to worries such as these, some four-dimensionalists reject perdurantism and accept the stage view (also known as exdurantism). (The view was first defended by Ted Sider [Sider 1996].) This is the third of the three main views of persistence. The stage view identifies the objects whose persistence we are interested in (including people and coffee mugs) with temporal parts, or stages. The stage theorist posits all the same objects as the perdurantist. But on the stage view, it is the stages that persist over time, and that we refer to when we refer to ordinary objects. When someone uses your name, they refer to a stage. Which stage they refer to depends on when they use the name. Some think that the stage view's solution to the problem of temporary intrinsics combines the advantages of the perdurantist solution with the advantages of the endurantist solution. In the stage view, there is no contradiction, because the incompatible intrinsic properties are had by different things, namely different stages. But it is still the persisting objects themselves that (directly) have the intrinsic properties, because the persisting objects *are* stages.

Of course, the stage view also faces problems. Perhaps most importantly, is it even a view of persistence? Persistence, we have said, is existence over time. But in the stage view, the things we ordinarily think persist only exist at one time, strictly speaking. So where has the persistence gone? The stage theorist typically offers the following reply: While it is true that strictly speaking, you do not exist at other times, we rarely speak that strictly. The ordinary claim that you were once a child is true. It is true because there exist certain other stages appropriately related to you. These other stages are temporal counterparts of yours. (Exactly what relations these have to you is an important question in its own right. Typically, the answer involves causal and similarity relations.)

We have now surveyed the three main contenders for how to think of the way things persist in time. Though less commonly than the metaphysical models of time itself, these positions also play a role in the discussion about God and time. Let us now turn to that discussion.

3 God Beyond Time

Recall that broadly speaking, there are two rival views of God's relationship to time: divine timelessness and divine temporality. As might be expected given the long history of the topic, there are a variety of views that fall under either heading.[5]

To begin with, note that it is not advisable to think of these positions as lying on a spectrum. The reason is that this suggests that being in spacetime, or being temporal, is something that comes in degrees, which is a substantial assumption. But it is certainly true to say that there are a variety of versions of divine timelessness, and of divine temporality. Sometimes it will be difficult to say in which camp a given view is best included. What matters is not the label, but each view's individual merits.

In this section, we take a closer look at divine timelessness and the reasons why one might accept it. The rough idea is that God is outside of time and does not experience things in succession. Rather, all things are experienced by God in a timeless ("eternal") present. Historically, this view has dominated in both philosophy and theology. We'll focus on the following versions: Pure Atemporalism, Stump and Kretzmann's view, Brian Leftow's view, and Robert Pasnau's view (which, as we will see, could arguably be classified as a temporal view instead). We'll then consider some arguments for divine timelessness from physics, metaphysics, and theology.

The first version of divine timelessness to consider, Pure Atemporalism, is one that may not have any official defenders (though Brian Leftow attributes something like this view to Maimonides and Schleiermacher [Leftow 2005]). It is perhaps most notable for its conceptual purity. It says, quite simply, that God is atemporal. God is not in spacetime, and God's life does not have any temporal features. Leftow further characterizes the view as one according to which God's relationship to time does not differ from that of abstract entities. The pressure to move away from this view arises from the fact that the God of

---

[5] Sections 3 and 4 contain developments of many ideas that first appeared in the SEP article "Eternity in Christian Thought" (Deng 2018b).

Western theism is a person who interacts with temporal beings. One influential attempt to do justice to this fact is the one by Eleonore Stump and Norman Kretzmann (e.g., Stump and Kretzmann 1981, 1987, 1992). Their view is based on the following four claims:

(1)   A timeless being has life. This assumption distinguishes a timeless being from abstract entities, like numbers or sets.

(2)   The life of a timeless being is without limit and cannot be limited, so, for example, it cannot begin or end.

(3)   The life of a timeless being therefore involves a special sort of atemporal duration.

(4)   A timeless being possesses its life all at once, completely.

This view, and Stump and Kretzmann's arguments for it, have been very widely discussed. They base it on Boethius, who is one of the *loci classici* for divine timelessness (*Consolation*, V.VI, transl. by Stewart et al. 1973): "Eternity [...] is the whole, simultaneous, and perfect possession of boundless life."

How should we understand (4)? There are at least two claims implicit here. The being in question does not experience succession – that is, for the being, things do not happen one after the other. And, its life's events do not succeed one another either. Since change requires succession, this latter claim implies that a timeless being does not change.

The challenge for Stump and Kretzmann is now to find a way to think of the timeless being as nonetheless "presently alive" in some sense, and of the being's life events as still "simultaneous" in some sense, both with each other and (even more importantly) with events and beings in time. The way they propose to accommodate this is as follows. First, define a timeless present (or, in their terminology, an eternal present) to be an infinitely extended, pastless and futureless duration. "Temporal simultaneity" is occurrence or existence at the same time, while "Eternal simultaneity" is occurrence or existence at the same timeless present. The key notion is "Eternal-Temporal simultaneity," or ET-simultaneity. This is simultaneity between eternal and temporal items.

How could that be the case? First, define an "eternal present" to be an infinitely extended, pastless, futureless duration (strictly speaking, on the terminology used here, it should be "timeless present," but "eternal present" is the more established term). Then let Temporal Simultaneity ("T-simultaneity") be existence/occurrence at the same time, and let Eternal Simultaneity ("E-simultaneity") be existence/occurrence at the same eternal present. Each involves only one mode of existence, namely either the temporal or the eternal.

ET-simultaneity, by contrast, relates items in different modes of existence, one temporal, and one eternal.

Let "x" and "y" range over entities and events. [...]

(ET) For every x and every y, x and y are ET-simultaneous if and only if:

i.   either x is eternal and y is temporal, or vice versa; and
ii. for some observer, A, in the unique eternal reference frame, x and y are both present – that is, either x is eternally present and y is observed as temporally present, or vice versa; and
iii. for some observer, B, in one of the infinitely many temporal reference frames, x and y are both present – that is, either x is observed as eternally present and y is temporally present, or vice versa. (Stump and Kretzmann 1981, 439)

Stump and Kretzmann elaborate on this in terms of an image of two parallel lines, with the lower one representing time, and the upper one representing eternity. Suppose presentness is represented by a light. In terms reminiscent of the moving spotlight view, they describe the temporal present as moving along the lower line, illuminating each time in turn. The upper line, however is different: it is lit all at once, representing the eternal present.

Recall that ET-simultaneity is supposed to help show that items in the lower line in some sense can be simultaneous with items in the upper line. Each time in the lower line is lit up in turn by the temporal present, and when it is so lit up, it is then ET-simultaneous with the whole of the upper line. However, this fact of ET-simultaneity between each time and the whole of eternity holds only "from the viewpoint of that time," and in particular it does not hold "from the viewpoint of eternity," from which instead the entire lower line is "lit up." For Stump and Kretzmann, "from the viewpoint of eternity" each time "insofar as [it] is temporally present" is ET-simultaneous with all of eternity (Stump and Kretzmann 1992, 475).

As we will see shortly, there are many points in this description and in the definition of ET-simultaneity about which one can raise legitimate questions. Before considering these, however, it is worth pointing out how the view is intended to solve a pressing problem for any view of this kind. Here is the problem in Anthony Kenny's words:

> But, on St. Thomas' view, my typing of this paper is simultaneous with the whole of eternity. Again, on his view, the great fire of Rome is simultaneous with the whole of eternity. Therefore, while I type these very words, Nero fiddles heartlessly on. (Kenny 1979, 38–9)

Stump and Kretzmann build ET-simultaneity so as to avoid this problem by fiat. Two items can, by definition, only be ET-simultaneous if one is temporal and the other eternal. Since nothing is both temporal and eternal, ET-simultaneity never holds between an item and itself. So, a fortiori, it is not the case that ET-simultaneity is reflexive. For similar reasons, and crucially, ET-simultaneity is also not transitive: it is not the case that whenever the relation holds between items x and y, and between items y and z, that it also holds between x and z. In fact, whenever it holds between x and y, and between y and z, it does not hold between x and z. It cannot, since x and z are then of the same kind (either both temporal or both eternal).

As a result, Kenny's problem is avoided. After all, the problem arises because one assumes that simultaneity is transitive (as well as symmetric): Kenny's typing is simultaneous with eternity, and so is the great fire of Rome. So (assuming symmetry) Kenny's typing is simultaneous with eternity, and eternity is simultaneous with the great fire of Rome; therefore, by transitivity, Kenny's typing is simultaneous with the great fire of Rome, and similarly for all other temporal events. Obviously, this implication is troublesome, because it is not the case that all things in time are simultaneous, as defenders of divine timelessness would want to acknowledge. That's why it is crucial to build in non-transitivity.

The problem nicely reflects the difficult balancing act that a theist, and in particular, a defender of divine timelessness, has to engage in. On the one hand, God is transcendent and sees all; on the other, God is in some sense present to each of us at all times, and to the world at each moment of its history. The challenge is to combine these ideas, while obliterating neither God's eternality, understood here as timelessness, nor the world's temporality.

Let us now return to the question of how to understand ET-simultaneity and associated notions. What, for example, is an atemporal duration? One might argue (Fitzgerald 1985; also Craig 1999; Nelson 1987; Helm 1988, 35) that there are certain formal features that characterize durations, like other extensions, that seem to be absent in the case of "atemporal duration." For example, it should be possible for different particulars to possess the same or different amounts of a given extension. Yet, it does not seem like that is the case with the eternal present. How then is it an infinitely extended duration at all?

In response, Stump and Kretzmann have argued that such features characterize only some kinds of duration, not all. In particular, they maintain that atemporal duration, like certain other kinds of temporal duration, is not divisible, and therefore does not exhibit the formal features mentioned (Stump and Kretzmann 1987, 1992). In order to substantiate this claim, they make use of the notion of a specious present, a notion that has its natural home in discussions about temporal experience (though there is a controversy surrounding the term and its usefulness today; for further reading, see the further references in Section 2). The term "specious present" is originally due to E. R. Clay, but it was made famous by William James. It refers to something like the temporal duration that some think is directly perceived in a single perception. Those who believe in it tend to think that temporal experience has a temporally extended content. In James's own words: "[T]he prototype of all conceived times is the specious present, the short duration of which we are immediately and incessantly sensible [. . .] We are constantly aware of a certain duration – the specious present – varying from a few seconds to probably not more than a minute, and this duration (with its content perceived as having one part earlier and another part later) is the original intuition of time" (James 1890).

How is the notion of the specious present relevant here? Stump and Kretzmann want to say that the specious present is a temporal extension that is not divisible. Their aim is to thereby support the claim that atemporal duration may still be a kind of duration, even if it too is not divisible and therefore satisfies none of the formal features of extension.

Consider the specious present – for example, the specious present during which a mother hears her son yell for help as he flies off his skateboard. The specious present is different from the metaphysical temporal present in being extended. It takes time, however little, for the mother to apprehend and process the various sounds that constitute the utterance "help," identify the utterance as her son's, and understand it. That time is, of course, conceptually divisible, but only into parts of that time, not into parts of the mother's specious present, which is characterized by her hearing her son yell for help. She may pick up theoretically distinguishable component sounds in conceptually divisible parts of the time underlying her specious present, but in none of those parts does she hear her son yell for help. Nor does she successively acquire each individual sound, remember it, and then integrate her short-term memories to produce in herself the experience of hearing "help." Reflections on the ludicrousness of such an account contributed to the original introduction of the notion of a specious present. The specious present, then, seems to be an instance of something that is both extended and conceptually indivisible as such (Stump and Kretzmann 1992, 468).

Stump and Kretzmann go on to say that there are other reasons to think the notion of a specious present fits well in this context. Following William Alston (Alston 1984; see also Leftow 1991), they recommend thinking of the eternal present as God's specious present, covering all of time. Michael Rea and Michael Murray make a similar point:

> [Y]our friend speaks to you and, though your experience of her action is surely divisible into experiences of parts of her action – bits of sound and perceived movement on her part and so on – it is not at all divisible into experiences of infinitesimal parts of her actions. The smallest units of your experience are, again, temporally thick. They have duration, even though all of their parts are, as it were, present to you all at once. This sort of temporally thick experience of the present is what people refer to as (experience of) the "specious present." And the idea underlying the doctrine of divine eternity is that God's life is sort of like an infinitely thick specious present. (Rea and Murray 2008, 41/2)

It would be less fruitful to speculate about the general merits of this analogy, than to examine the particular use to which Stump and Kretzmann want to put it. The problem is that, as Rea and Murray's exposition makes clear, there are a number of ways in which the term "specious present" can be understood. In particular, it could be taken to refer to the experience of a temporally extended content, or else to that temporally extended content itself. In the former case, we might say the term refers to the act of apprehending the duration, whereas in the latter, it refers to what is apprehended. This matters for Stump and Kretzmann's purposes, because their argument is in danger of trading on this ambiguity. What is temporally extended is the object of the awareness, the content of the act of awareness. That content, by the same token, appears to be capable of conceptual division and to contain different sub-durations of various lengths. It is the act that is not, perhaps, so divisible – but the act is also not temporally extended (Oppy 1998 contains a related critique of Leftow's use of the notion).[6]

We have seen that the divine timelessness theorist needs to walk a fine line in order to obliterate neither God's timeless eternity nor the world's temporality. Another way in which this difficulty manifests itself in Stump and Kretzmann's proposal is that one might well wonder what it can mean for an eternally present entity to observe something as being temporally present, or vice versa (Lewis 1984; also Nelson 1987; Padgett 1992, 69; Swinburne 1993). How does this observational contact work, and how can it avoid bringing either the eternal into the temporal realm or vice versa? *Prima facie*, a temporal entity's observation of something as being eternal is an event, namely the same event as that eternal entity's being observed by the temporal entity.

Partly in response to these and related difficulties, Stump and Kretzmann also offer a revised version of the definition of ET-simultaneity:

(ET′) For every x and every y, x and y are ET-simultaneous if and only if

---

[6] Stump and Kretzmann have also pointed to the use of analogical predication elsewhere in theology to justify their use of the term "extension" here. See Rogers 1994 for further discussion.

(i) either x is eternal and y is temporal, or vice versa (for convenience, let x be eternal and y temporal); and

(ii) with respect to some A in the unique eternal reference frame, x and y are both present – i.e., (a) x is in the eternal present with respect to A, (b) y is in the temporal present, and (c) both x and y are situated with respect to A in such a way that A can enter into direct and immediate causal relations with each of them and (if capable of awareness) can be directly aware of each of them; and

(iii) with respect to some B in one of the infinitely many temporal reference frames, x and y are both present – i.e., (a) x is in the eternal present, (b) y is at the same time as B, and (c) both x and y are situated with respect to B in such a way that B can enter into direct and immediate causal relations with each of them and (if capable of awareness) can be directly aware of each of them. (Stump and Kretzmann 1992, 477–8)

While at first sight, this may seem to *provide* an answer to the question of how observation can cross the temporal-timelessness divide, on closer inspection one may well worry that it in fact *relies* on such an answer (Leftow 1991, 173; also Fales 1997).

Furthermore, one has to wonder how useful it can be to borrow notions from (some presentations of) special relativity in this context. Stump and Kretzmann intend to show, with this talk of reference frames and observers, that the difficulties with ET-simultaneity are "by no means unique" and "cannot be assumed to be difficulties in the concepts of ET-simultaneity or of eternity themselves" (Stump and Kretzmann 1981, 439). But it is doubtful whether allusions to special relativity play this role. Stump and Kretzmann present special relativity as involving the finding that simultaneity is a three-place relation, which they interpret as a response to a threat of incoherence of two distant events being both "simultaneous [...] and not simultaneous" (Stump and Kretzmann 1981, 437). But it is not being two- or three-place that makes the notion of ET-simultaneity objectionable. It is that the ingredients themselves of that notion, such as the notions of an eternal present, and of a unique eternal reference frame, remain mysterious. The situation is rather different in the case of special relativity (Fales 1997; also Padgett 1992, 71; Craig 2009).

It may be useful to pause here and recall what is at stake in this discussion. Whether or not God can causally interact with our spatiotemporal world is, as Fales (1997) argues, central to how one views the relation between science and religion. And while divine timelessness is, at least in philosophy, less widely defended today than it used to be, it still represents an approach with much intuitive appeal. So it is of no small import whether causal interactions between a timelessly eternal God and our world are conceivable. If they are not, it seems that there can be no empirical confirmation or disconfirmation of the existence of a timeless God, nor can a timeless God be active in our lives, influencing the course of world history.

Are there any other approaches to divine timelessness that may fare better? Another influential version is due to Brian Leftow. Leftow bases his view on the Anselmian idea that temporal beings are not only in time but, together with God, in timeless eternity.

To begin with, consider God's relation not to time, but to space. Is God in this room, literally? The traditional theistic stance has been that God has no spatial location. Presumably then, there are no spatial distance relations between spatial things and God. Leftow infers from this the "Zero Thesis": the distance between God and any thing in space is zero (Leftow 1991, 222).

By this reasoning, one is led to suspect that the distance between God and any spatial thing always is zero. So nothing ever moves with respect to God. If we now accept the further claim that all change supervenes on motion (in particular, the motion of small particles composing the changing objects), it follows that there is no change with respect to God (Leftow 1991, 227). Like Stump and Kretzmann, Leftow here imports vocabulary from the physics of motion and asserts that in God's "eternal frame of reference" nothing changes and all events are simultaneous. God and all spatial things share this frame of reference, in which God's actions and their effects are simultaneous. Leftow also argues that eternity is something like a time, at which all these things happen simultaneously. By contrast, in temporal reference frames, God's actions occur in eternity, but their effects are not simultaneous.

The problem with Leftow's argument for the Zero Thesis is straightforward: from the fact that there is no spatial distance between two things, it does not follow that the spatial distance between them is zero. In fact, this is a very peculiar inference to make. It involves inferring from the fact that a relation does not hold between two items that it does hold between those items.

The further elements of Leftow's view build on the debate between A- and B-theorists in the metaphysics of time (see Section 2). Recall that according to the B-theory, all times exist (eternalism), and there is a complete tenseless description of temporal reality. That is, at the fundamental level, there are only tenseless facts, concerning which events happen when, and how they are temporally related to one another. These facts do not change, so there is no robust passage of time. The tenseless description, then, does not mention any tensed facts such as that it is 12:00 now, or that it was 12:01 a moment ago and that it is now 12:02.

Recall also that the A-theory, in its various guises, denies either eternalism or the claim that there is a complete tenseless description of reality. For an A-theorist, one time is metaphysically privileged in some way, and the gaining and shedding of this privilege is what makes it the case that time robustly passes.

Leftow elaborates on his view by coining distinctions that are intended to be reminiscent of the A versus B distinction. However, the distinctions he introduces are somewhat more difficult to grasp than the A versus B distinction itself. He defines "A-occurring" to be occurring now, and "B-occurring" to be occurring at a certain temporal location t that is now. The idea is that B-occurring entails A-occurring (if something occurs at a temporal B-location t that is now, it occurs now), but not vice versa (something can occur now without occurring at a temporal B-location t that is now). He also defines A-simultaneity as occurring "at the same now," and B-simultaneity as "having the same temporal B-location in some B-series."

The main purpose of these definitions is to allow us to say that "the A-simultaneity that obtains between a timeless God and temporal entities is univocal with the A-simultaneity that obtains between temporal entities" (Leftow 1991, 239). Unlike in the Stump and Kretzmann view, then, the simultaneity between God in timeless eternity and temporal things is the same kind of simultaneity that obtains just between temporal things, rather than a *sui generis* kind of a relation (as is ET-simultaneity). However, it is hardly surprising that the definitions allow one to say that. After all, something similar is stipulated by Leftow to begin with: "[L]et us so understand 'now' that occurring now does not entail having a position in a B-series of earlier and later events. That is, let us in effect take 'now' and 'occurring now' as primitive terms univocally applicable to temporal and eternal or timeless things" (Leftow 1991, 239).

One thing that's interesting about Leftow's version of divine timelessness is that it makes explicit some ideas about a connection to the A versus B debate that may well play a role in other proposals too. As we have seen, for Leftow all things in timeless eternity are simultaneous – A-simultaneous, to be precise. But Leftow also sometimes describes timeless eternity as consisting of different B-series corresponding to different temporal frames of reference (Leftow 1991, 239). Yet, a B-series is a sequence of events succeeding one another. In a related context, Leftow coins the notion of Quasi-Temporal Eternality (QTE; Leftow 1991, 120–2), which is his take on atemporal duration. For him, an atemporal duration has no parts but it does contain different points, which, in some sense, are temporally related to one another as earlier-later. Nonetheless, he insists, they do not stand in a succession relation.

The way to make sense of this juxtaposition of ideas, according to Leftow, is to recall the B-theory of time. We are to understand QTE, and life in timeless eternity, by considering life in a B-theoretic universe. In particular, eternity is like life in B-time except without an illusion of time's robustly passing. Take away the illusion of passage in a B-theoretic universe, and what you end up with is the experience of a QTE being.

But this is puzzling. A QTE being's life is a life in which all is experienced at once. So it is a life in which no succession is experienced. But the B-theory posits succession. It just does not posit (robust) temporal passage. An experience of succession is veridical, on the B-theory. So, *pace* Leftow, we cannot understand a QTE being's life along the lines of life in a B-theoretic universe without the illusion of (robust) temporal passage.

It is worth pausing here to compare this to Laurie Paul's defense of illusionism on the B-theory (see Section 2). Effectively, the idea there is that without an illusion of (robust) temporal passage, in the B-theory, a subject would be left with an experience of discreteness, or gappiness. I suggested there that there is no reason to think this, since B-theorists are not committed to the claim that time is discrete (much less that it has gaps that are somehow themselves in time). A similar criticism is applicable here: Leftow effectively maintains that without an illusion of (robust) temporal passage, on the B-theory, a subject would be left with an experience of only a single time point (which can then be likened to an atemporal now). But *prima facie*, if the B-theory contains succession, then, without an illusion of temporal passage, a subject in B-time is left with an experience of succession.

However, there *is* a view of time in the vicinity of the B-theory that is relevant to Leftow's purposes. Despite the view's strangeness, it is worth examining, even if just in order to clarify what the B-theory does not say. I've suggested elsewhere that this view of time can offer some quasi-religious comfort even to atheists (Deng 2015).

We can arrive at the view in question – for reasons that will become clear, we might call it the eternal present* view – by taking some of the metaphors that get used in connection with the B-theory too seriously, so to speak. Usually, it is important to keep in mind that in the B-theory, times are not really "out there" in any literal sense. They are not themselves (in) some kind of space; time is like space only in very particular respects. For example, all times exist, just like all spatial locations do, and no time is metaphysically privileged, just like no spatial location is. Terms like "past" and "future" express temporal perspectives, just like "here" and "there" express spatial perspectives. So on the B-theory, it is not literally the case that all times exist "at once," in a *totum simul*. Rather, all times exist, *simpliciter*; all times exist, full stop.[7]

Now suppose we think of times as literally "out there," as quasi-spatial in some sense. All times, in this view, exist "at once" – but this "at once" cannot refer to simultaneity or the present in our ordinary sense since we are talking about all of our times standing in this relation. Instead of quotation marks, let us use a "*" and say that all times, on this view, exist at once*. The resulting view, then, says that our temporal dimension is in fact quasi-spatial, and that all these quasi-spatial times exist at once* in a second temporal realm. Again, let us call that the eternal present* view of time.

The eternal present* view is not easy to make sense of, or to defend (what licenses calling the second temporal* realm "temporal*" at all?). In that view, it is almost the case that time itself persists in a second temporal* realm; except that this realm is not extended, but rather pointlike. This view of time has clear affinities with the view of eternity implicit in Leftow's proposal.

While it is important to keep in mind that the eternal present* view is not the B-theory as such, some B-theoretic views do have a certain similarity with the eternal present* view. For example, many illusionist B-theorists think that due to the pervasive illusion of robust passage, we perceive the world to be very different from the way it really is. Some even think to a significant extent, we project motion and change onto the world (Le Poidevin 2007). On such a B-theoretic view, the appearances are deceiving – reality is rather less changeable and dynamic than it seems ordinarily. This is somewhat similar to the eternal present* view, in the following way. On the eternal present* view too, reality is very much unlike it seems, because the second temporal* realm consists of something like a single time* point – a single eternal present*. If this realm is more fundamental than our ordinary temporal realm, then this, in a way, is how things really are. In a way, temporality – in the sense of a succession of times, as well as of a past, present, or future – is an illusion. I've argued that this view of time can, to an extent, offer comfort in the face of loss even to atheists (Deng 2015).[8] It is not surprising to find that it has affinities with versions of divine

---

[7] It would be perfectly legitimate for the reader to question what it means for times to exist, *simpliciter* (for more on this point, see Deng 2018a).

[8] Shortly after the death of his friend Michele Besso, Einstein remarked: "Now he has also gone ahead of me a little in departing from this peculiar world. This means nothing. For us believing physicists, the division between past, present and future has only the significance of a stubbornly persistent illusion." "parenthesis". Should read as: "Illusion." ("Nun ist er mir auch mit dem Abschied von dieser sonderbaren Welt ein wenig vorausgegangen. Dies bedeutet nichts. Für uns gläubige Physiker hat die Scheidung zwischen Vergangenheit, Gegenwart und Zukunft nur die Bedeutung einer wenn auch hartnäckigen Illusion.") (Einstein 1972, 538; my translation)

timelessness. At least it is not surprising if one thinks that one of the functions of the theistic worldview is to provide comfort.

The final view we will consider in this section is one by Robert Pasnau. One reason we consider it is that it represents an interesting recent contribution to the God and Time debate that is rooted in other areas of philosophy and the history of philosophy. Pasnau sets out to delineate a version of eternality that is "not complete timelessness" but rather "all-at-once existence." (One could make a case for treating this as a version of divine temporality instead of divine timelessness: "There is something quite unattractive about the picture according to which God created space and time and yet does not – perhaps even cannot – exist within it. Intuitively, one would expect God to exist at every place and every time, rather than at no place and no time" (Pasnau 2011, 22). But the account nevertheless shares enough features with other divine timelessness views that it belongs in this section. This is particularly clear with regard to the stance taken on the second issue distinguished in the introduction, regarding (a)temporal features of God's experience. In any case, keep in mind that these classifications do not much matter except for practical purposes.) Pasnau takes this view to be a historically important and intrinsically plausible conception of eternality that is in danger of getting overlooked in the modern discussion. He starts out by offering the following definitions:

> A *temporal* entity, as I will use the term here, exists at one or more times and, unless it exists for just an instant, exists through time. It coexists – that is, exists simultaneously – with other entities existing at the same time.
>
> An *atemporal* entity, on my usage, is one that is not temporal. It does not exist in time, in the sense that it does not exist at any time and so, a fortiori, does not exist through time. It cannot be said to exist simultaneously with, or before, or after any other entity.
>
> A *merechronic* entity partly exists at some instant in time, but also existed or will exist at other times, and does not wholly exist at any one time.
>
> A *holochronic* entity is one that is not merechronic. It exists as a whole, all at once, for all of its existence, and does not partly exist at different times.
>
> (Pasnau 2011, 11)

Pasnau acknowledges that the merechronicity-holochronicity distinction contains echoes of the modern distinction between enduring and perduring objects, as well as of the scholastic distinction between "successive" and "permanent" entities. Indeed, one of the conclusions to be derived from the discussion is that both of these aim at something like the former. But since this is to be a conclusion, rather than an assumption, we are to understand the merechronicity-holochronicity distinction without reference to the other two.

Readers familiar with the modern debate about persistence may well find this difficult to do, since merechronicity, for instance, is most straightforwardly interpreted as never being wholly present and persisting by having temporal parts. Holochronicity correspondingly might be understood as being either atemporal, or instantaneous and non-persisting, or enduring – being wholly present at each time one exists and not having temporal parts. Things are not helped when Pasnau goes on to explain what it is to persist by having temporal parts and then says that "to have temporal parts in this way" (the usual way) "is to be a merechronic entity" (Pasnau 2011, 12). This makes it very tempting to understand the new distinction in light of the distinction between enduring and perduring entities.

However, Pasnau then goes on to say that merechronicity is a kind of intrinsic change, a "part-by-part traversal of a complete life." One implication of this is that any entity that does not change intrinsically is holochronic.

But this should give us pause. If, as it seems we must, we think of merechronicity with the help of our prior understanding of perduring entities, why can a merechronic entity not stay the same intrinsically? It would then have temporal parts that exist at different times but that have all the same intrinsic features. So it is not clear that one should think of any entity that does not change intrinsically as holochronic. More importantly, it is still not clear what holochronicity is. An atemporal entity has to be holochronic, since being temporal is built into the definition of merechronicity, and the two kinds of chronicity are by definition exhaustive. A holochronic entity may or may not be atemporal. But which temporal entities count as holochronic? Do all enduring entities count? Do instantaneous entities?

Pasnau instead focuses on the following question: Is eternality just illimitable, temporally extended, holochronic existence? Or does eternality require atemporality in addition to holochronicity?

He then argues for two claims (though he does not distinguish them): (1) Boethius may have had holochronicity in mind when describing God's relationship to time, and (2) this conception of God's relationship to time is plausible, that is, it is plausible to think that God's eternality amounts to merely being holochronic without being atemporal. The main argument for both (1) and (2) is contained in the following passage. Note that Pasnau treats the term "timeless" differently from our usage here; for him it effectively just means eternal, where eternality is the notion to be fleshed out. So (2), for Pasnau, is the claim that holochronicity is one plausible way to spell out what God's timelessness (or eternality) amounts to:

> It is certainly not unreasonable to suppose [. . .] that Boethius is committed to God's atemporality. On this reading of [Boethius], one would have a ready explanation of why he talks about holochronicity, since holochronicity follows trivially from atemporality. But there is another way to read [Boethius]. Mere holochronicity itself might be considered a kind of time-lessness. Since such a being is entirely changeless, without even a distinct past or future, it fails to be located in time in the usual way. Hence it might be argued that Boethius's denial of God's being located in time should be understood merely as the denial of God's merechronicity, not as the claim that God is entirely outside of time. I am not taking a position on whether this is the most plausible reading – we would need to look at more texts – only that we should be alert to the conceptual room here for different sorts of timelessness, including illimitable holochronicity, rather than atemporality. (Pasnau 2011, 14)

Presumably more textual evidence could at most provide reasons to accept (1) (an exegetical claim), not (2). Moreover, it is hard to feel very confident of (2) on the basis of these remarks. As mentioned, it is still not clear how to understand holochronicity, nor is it clear why holochronicity implies change-lessness. For instance, if we take temporal holochronic entities to be enduring entities, presumably some holochronic entities do change. Certainly there is nothing in the definition of endurantism to rule out that some enduring entities change.

Moreover, it is difficult to assess the claim that holochronicity amounts to a kind of timelessness. If holochronicity is being an enduring entity, it is unclear why that should have anything to do with timelessness in any sense. After all, endurantism is a view about how things in time persist through time. If holochronicity is being an instantaneous entity, that again has nothing to do with timelessness in any sense – an instantaneous entity is in time, namely at exactly one time. If holochronicity is or (somehow) implies being changeless, then that is not a *kind* of timelessness, though it may or may not *imply* time-lessness, in the sense of atemporality. Pasnau, however, seems to think change-lessness does not imply timelessness in the sense of atemporality – he even thinks immutability (which is stronger) does not imply atemporality (Pasnau 2011, 15; we will return to this issue below).

In any case, that is not the kind of timelessness Pasnau is claiming for holochronicity. The claim is not that holochronicity is a kind of atemporality; the claim is that holochronicity is a different kind of timelessness. But what, then, is the kind of timelessness Pasnau is claiming for holochronicity? Without some idea of that, it is hard to fight off the suspicion that this is a merely verbal move: he is advocating calling changelessness "timelessness" instead. One could do the same with "instantaneous" – one could start calling all instantaneous entities timeless. But it is no doubt better just to call things by their actual names.

One might object that Pasnau tells us what kind of timelessness he is claiming for holochronicity, namely, not having a distinct past or future. But what does that mean? What is it for one's past and future not to be "distinct"? If it means not having a past or future, that just brings us back to being instantaneous, i.e., existing at exactly one time.

Pasnau elaborates on the notion of holochronicity using a comparison with the corresponding spatial notion, holenmericity.

> A *meremeric* entity partly exists at some location in space, but also partly exists at some other location in space. It is an extended entity, having part outside of part.
>
> A *holenmeric* entity is one that is not meremeric. It exists as a whole, altogether, wherever it exists, and so lacks extended parts.
>
> (Pasnau 2011, 18)

Thus, just like holenmeric entities exist as a whole wherever they exist, so holochronic entities exist as a whole whenever they exist. This again suggests that we should equate temporal holochronicity with endurance. After all, enduring entities are ones that persist by being wholly present at each time they exist. However, as we have seen, that interpretation makes trouble for Pasnau's claim that holochronicity is a kind of timelessness, and for his claim that holochronicity implies changelessness. In addition, it is contrary to the stated aim of starting out with an independent understanding of holochronicity, and to derive a link to the persistence issue from the discussion.

One more point is worth noting. Pasnau suggests that a holochronicity-based view of God's eternality need not force one to see ordinary objects as merechronic, as perduring. It allows one to maintain that God's way of being in time is properly special, even while one holds on to the claim that ordinary objects (like ourselves) endure too, and are therefore holochronic too. One way to do this is as follows, according to Pasnau. One can claim that while ordinary objects endure, their lives perdure. By contrast, God is identical with God's life. So in God's case, even the life endures, so to speak. *Both* are holochronic. (Pasnau also makes a connection with the medieval distinction between permanent and successive entities at this point.)

The point to note about this is that the question of persistence is a question about how things, i.e., objects, including persons, exist through time. It is not about events (such as lives). Thus, a discussion of whether or not an entity's life endures or perdures may well rest on a misunderstanding.

We have now surveyed some approaches to divine timelessness. For other versions see, for example, Helm 1988, 2001; Yates 1990; Rogers 2000, 2007.

Now, why might one want to uphold divine timelessness? We will consider six arguments in favor of the view. One is based mostly on physics, three mostly on theology, and two mostly on metaphysics.

Let us start with the physics-based argument. Recall that contemporary physics enters the God and time discussion in a number of different places. First, it is highly relevant to the merits of various metaphysical views about time. Second, some versions of divine timelessness contain analogies to special relativity. And now we encounter a third connection, also to relativity theory. One can reason as follows (e.g., Leftow 1991, 272):

(1) God is an immaterial substance.
(2) Immaterial substances are not in space. So,
(3) God is not in space. (It is usually seen as a traditional theistic commitment that God is not in space, though see Pasnau (2011, 19) for a different view of the tradition and, e.g., Inman 2016 for modern dissent.) But,
(4) according to relativity theory, anything that is in time is also in space. Therefore,
(5) if relativity theory is correct (in essentials), then God is not in time.
(6) Relativity theory is correct (in essentials). So,
(7) God is not in time. So,
(8) God is timeless.

The motivation behind (5) is that, as we saw in Section 2, in relativity theory there is no unique decomposition of spacetime into space at times.[9]

The next three arguments have a rather different flavor. Suppose you think that God is the most perfect, or the greatest possible being. Then you might wonder: Isn't timeless existence a more perfect mode of existence than being in time? Isn't it greater for a being to be outside of time? If so, then it follows from God's being the most perfect being that God is timeless.

But why should you think timelessness a "more perfect" mode of existence than temporal existence? Consider, for instance, the enjoyment of music, which seems to be open only to temporal beings. More generally, why think that it is temporality as such that tends to make our lives less than perfect? There are, after all, many aspects of the lives of temporal creatures such as ourselves that contribute to making those lives less than perfect, and many of these aspects would presumably be absent in the case of God. God's life, even if temporal,

---

[9] The "in essentials" is needed because relativity theory is not the final world in physics. Physicists have yet to find the prospective theory of quantum gravity, which would combine the principles of both relativity theory and quantum theory. For our purposes, what matters is that that prospective theory is unlikely to reverse the transition from prerelativistic to relativistic physics by reinstating a unique decomposition of spacetime into space at times.

would still not involve gain or loss in the way that our lives, and the lives of non-human animals, do. Suppose one abstracts away from the ordinary accompaniments of the passage of time, such as ageing, loss, and dying. And suppose one also abstracts away from the usual epistemic limitations of temporal beings, namely the fact that we perceive only roughly the present, and that we know much less about the future than the past. After all, none of this would be the case for God. Is the resulting mode of temporal existence still "less than perfect," just because it involves experiencing things one at a time? It is not so clear (cf. Mullins 2014).

The idea that God is the most perfect being, or the greatest possible being, has been a central one in some strands of theology (perfect being theology). Many have tried to take it as their starting point for investigating God's nature. The next two arguments do just this; and unlike the previous argument, there is an intermediate step in each (that God is simple, and that God is immutable, respectively).

(1)   If God is the most perfect being, then God is simple.
(2)   If God is simple, then God is timeless.
(3)   God is the most perfect being. Therefore,
(4)   God is timeless.

Alternatively (and this argument we will consider in more detail below):

(5)   If God is the most perfect being, then God is immutable.
(6)   If God is immutable, then God is timeless.
(7)   God is the most perfect being. Therefore, (4) God is timeless.

Let us consider the connection between timelessness and immutability a little more carefully. One of the first questions to ask here is what is meant by "immutable." Recall from Section 2 that an intrinsic property is one that objects have just in virtue of how they are in themselves, not how they are in relation to other things. An intrinsic change is a change in intrinsic properties. Suppose that by "immutable" we mean incapable of undergoing intrinsic change. Let us call the claim that God is immutable in this sense the doctrine of divine immutability, or DDI (Leftow 2005, 2016; cf. Craig 2009). Then, is this last argument (the one following "Alternatively") persuasive?

Since the argument is valid, the main question is whether or not its premises are true. Premise (6) is the most relevant for our purposes. Is it the case that simply being in time necessarily brings with it some intrinsic changes? Is simply growing older – even without any of the usual accompaniments of growingolder, without the biological ageing process – an intrinsic change? That is, is simply having been around for longer than you had been previously a change in an intrinsic property? Suppose it is. Then as long as one is not instantaneous (as we assume God is not), being in time entails undergoing an intrinsic change, so that DDI entails that God is timeless. But suppose that growing older is an extrinsic change. The many accompanying changes (such as changes in hair color or waist circumference) may be intrinsic, but perhaps growing older by itself is not. After all, growing older involves changes in such properties as being a certain number of years separated from one's birth, which arguably is a property one has in virtue of how one is in relation to something else (one's birth). Then there is no direct entailment from DDI to divine timelessness.

However, there is another way to argue from DDI to divine timelessness, based on Aquinas (as reconstructed in Leftow 2005):

(1) A thing is temporal only if it can change intrinsically, or change its place, or has parts which can change places, or can begin and cease to exist.

(2) Whatever is essentially not in space cannot change place or have parts which do.

(3) So whatever is intrinsically immutable, not in space, and without beginning or end of existence is not temporal.

(4) God is essentially not in space.

(5) Whatever is intrinsically immutable does not begin or cease to exist.

(6) God is intrinsically immutable.

(7) So God is not temporal – his life is not located in time. (Leftow 2005, 62/63)

Leftow maintains that Scripture by itself rules out God's ceasing or beginning to exist, and that (4) is part of "standard" Western theism. (However, as noted above, there are contemporary defenses of the view that God is in fact located in space [e.g., Inman 2016].) Much then depends on the merits of (1). If (1) is true, we can infer from DDI that God is timeless.

The final two arguments for divine timelessness have to do not with God's perfection, but with God's foreknowledge, or knowledge of the future. There are at least two quite different arguments in this vicinity. The first one goes like this. The only way to know about the future, to have complete knowledge of future contingent events, is to be outside of time; temporal beings do not have that kind of knowledge. But God is omniscient, so God is timeless. Of course, this will only have force for those who think God does have complete knowledge of future contingent events. Not all theists agree (exceptions include some Open Theists; see Section 4).

The second argument based on foreknowledge presents timelessness as a way to avoid a conflict between divine foreknowledge and genuine human freedom. Consider first how the conflict is thought to arise; this is known as the problem of theological fatalism (Rea and Murray 2008, 50). Suppose p is the proposition that you will read this book in 1,000 years' time. Suppose further that "t*" refers to a time 1,000 years ago, and "t" to the present time. Then one can reason as follows:

(1)   p was true at t*.

(2)   God is omniscient.

(3)   An omniscient being believes every true proposition and has no false beliefs.

(4)   Therefore: at t*, God believed that p was true. [From (1), (2), (3)]

(5)   Premise (4) entails that you read this book at t. (That is, it is impossible that premise (4) be true and you not read this book at t.)

(6)   No human being has ever had a choice about the truth of premise (4).

(7)   For any propositions p and q, if p is true and if p entails q, and if no human being has ever had a choice about the truth of p, then no human being has ever had a choice about the truth of q.

(8)   No human being – and so not even you – has ever had a choice about whether you read this book at t. [From (5), (6), (7)]

(9)   A person is free with respect to an action only if that person has a choice about whether or not to perform the action.

(10)   Therefore: though you read (that is, you are reading) this book at t, you do not do so freely. [From (8), (9)]

This then generalizes to all putatively free human actions, so that we seem forced to conclude that if there is an omniscient God, no human (or non-human animal) ever acts freely. This is the problem of theological fatalism, and one proposed solution is based on divine timelessness. The rough idea is that since God is outside of time, God somehow knows and believes things outside of time. That is, God did not believe anything 1,000 years ago (so (4) is false) because God does not believe things *at times*. However, it should be noted that it is by no means clear that this helps, since a very similar problem may well arise on timelessness views (Zagzebski 1991, ch. 2). Note also that there are other proposed solutions to the problem of theological fatalism that do not involve divine time-lessness. In a way, this is what one should have expected. After all, there is a strikingly similar secular argument for logical fatalism. That argument proceeds as follows:

(1)   p was true at t*.

(5′)   Premise (1) entails that you read this book at t. (That is, it is impossible that premise (1) be true though you do not read this book at t.)

(6')   No human being has ever had a choice about the truth of premise (1).

(7')   For any propositions p and q, if p is true and if p entails q, and if no human being has ever had a choice about the truth of p, then no human being has ever had a choice about the truth of q.

(8')   No human being – and so not even you – has, had, or ever will have a choice about whether you read this book at t.

(9)   A person is free with respect to an action only if that person has a choice about whether or not to perform the action.

(10)   Therefore: though you read (that is, you are reading) this book at t, you do not do so freely. One famous (Aristotelian) solution to this problem is to deny (1).

We have now discussed a number of versions of divine timelessness, and we have encountered a number of problems in each case. At the same time, we have seen that there are many arguments that friends of divine timelessness can make for their position from a variety of starting points, including physics, metaphysics, and theology. Let us now have a look at the opposing camp, which, as already been hinted, has been gaining favor in recent decades.

4 God in Time

Recall that temporal views say, roughly, that God is in time and experiences temporal succession. God exists at every time. God's eternality consists in there being no time at which God does not exist.

In a way, the more straightforwardly temporal one's view of God, the less there is to say about the view (at least insofar as the view's claims about God's relationship to time are concerned). Nonetheless, there are a variety of views to consider. Some of these could also be, and sometimes are, classified as "in-between" views; as before, the classifications do not really matter except for practical purposes. We'll start with Pure Temporalism, and then consider views by Alan Padgett, Garrett DeWeese, William Lane Craig, and Richard Swinburne. Then we'll encounter a number of arguments in favor of divine temporalism, one of which has traditionally been strongly linked to the A versus B debate in the metaphysics of time.

The first view we might call Pure Temporalism. This is sometimes ascribed to process theologians like Charles Hartshorne (Hartshorne 1947). If Pure Atemporalism was the view that God is in every respect atemporal (outside of spacetime, and not experiencing succession), then Pure Temporalism is the opposite, in the following sense. For a Pure Temporalist, the only way in which God's relationship to time differs from ours is in its infinite extent. God experiences succession, and God is in time – but God has lived through and will live through a non-finite past and future. Since the view does not go on to posit a different time for God than for us, it is arguably in tension with modern cosmology, since it seems to conflict with the claim that the universe has a finite past. From the theist's perspective, another disadvantage is that it may seem to leave God powerless in relation to time, so to speak. That is, it may suggest that God is somehow bound by or limited by time. The severity of this problem depends on the precise form that Pure Temporalism takes. A process theology version of Pure Temporalism is perhaps particularly susceptible to the problem, because it tends to emphasize the metaphysical ultimacy of time.

One central idea in the divine temporality literature is the idea that God is in a different time from ours ("divine time," "God's time," "metaphysical time"). Alan Padgett and Garrett DeWeese have both defended views like this (Padgett 1992, 2001; DeWeese 2002, 2004). Padgett claims that God is "relatively timeless," and DeWeese says that God is "omnitemporal." There are differences between the views, but both make this distinction between God's time and ours. Roughly, the idea is that physical time has an intrinsic metric, while metaphysical time, God's time, does not. Metaphysical time is "metrically amorphous." The reason is that the metrical properties of our time are due to regular occurrences, which in turn are due to the natural laws that govern events in physical time. With God's time, the situation is different; relatedly, God is not subject to the laws of nature. God experiences temporal succession, but this succession is of events within God's consciousness and of events constituting God's actions. These are not subject to laws of nature, so they do not ground any metrical properties for "metaphysical time." Nonetheless, God's now coincides with that of physical time.

Clearly, these claims are intended to move one away from Pure Temporalism, and away from any suspicion that God, by being temporal, becomes somehow "bound" by time or time's prisoner. The idea that God is not in our "measured" time is intended to help the divine temporalist avoid this.

Another claim that the divine temporalist may make use of for this purpose is that God is not negatively affected by the passage of time. We have already met this conceptual possibility, in the context of arguments for the claim that timelessness is a more perfect mode of existence than temporality. *Prima facie*, there do not seem to be any special difficulties in abstracting away from the usual accompaniments of the passage of time (ageing, dying). (Note that we need not mean by this a metaphysically robust passage of time; the same points could be made on the B-theory.) One can imagine God not to suffer gain or loss in the way that other persons do. In that case God would perhaps not be negatively affected by the passage of time.

There are a number of questions one might have about this kind of view. Why think that there are these two different kinds of time, and what makes it the case that the amorphous one is still a kind of time? The more the difference in kind between the two is emphasized, the more the view starts to resemble divine timelessness views. The label "metaphysical time" seemingly reflects a conviction, explicitly voiced by Padgett, that the time talked about in everyday speech is usually regarded as non-identical with the time investigated by philosophers of time, such as metaphysicians. The former is "the human time of our history and our universe," "the time of seconds, days, and centuries, the time of our space-time" (1992, 130), while the latter is an ontological category and hence time in "a strict sense." But that is not so, as far as modern metaphysicians are concerned. Their intention, at least, is to study the one thing that both ordinary people and philosophers (as well as physicists, psychologists, historians, etc.) talk about when they talk about time. So there is no default assumption of non-identity to fall back on in the philosophy of time.

Moreover, even if we knew what made God's time into a kind of time, and even if there were sufficient reason to suppose the two kinds of time existed, what would be the relation between the two? In particular, if God is in God's own time, does that mean he is not in ours? And if God is not in our time, then one might think the practical upshot is the same as if God was outside of time altogether. The interaction with the world that Scripture and religious practice seem to require depends on some relation to *our* time. Indeed, Padgett denies that God is not in our time. At least he says it is "philosophically acceptable" to say that God is in our time too (1992, 131). God is in our time, but God transcends that time. But what is it to transcend our time, and in addition how is being in one's own time either necessary or sufficient for transcendence? Padgett, unfortunately, does not answer these questions. He says three things about what it is to transcend time: it is to be the ground of time, it is to not be negatively affected by the passage of time, and it is to be relatively timeless. The third point does not help, since it is just another label for the view in question, in which God "transcends" our time by being in his own. The first two points do not really help either. The main reason is that either could hold without God's being in his own time at all. Why not just say that God is the ground of our physical time, and that God is not negatively affected by the passage of time, and leave it at that?

William Lane Craig's view is somewhat similar, but it involves a new twist in that Craig concludes that "God is timeless without creation and temporal subsequent to creation" (Craig 2000, 33). The question, though, is what "without" and "subsequent" mean here, if not before and after. Craig never really confronts this question, though he himself argues that they cannot mean that. If an entity is P before t and Q after t, then that entity is temporal throughout.

Craig's solution to this problem is "that 'prior' to creation there literally are no intervals of time [. . .] no earlier and later, no enduring through successive intervals and, hence, no waiting, no temporal becoming. This state would pass away, not successively, but as a whole, at the moment of creation, when time begins." And this state, he says, "looks suspiciously like a state of timelessness" (Craig 2000: 33). But this solution looks suspiciously like a restatement of the view. The problem was that we could only talk of a "before" in quotation marks. Yet we needed there to literally be such a before on the view in question (unless, that is, we decline to make literal sense of all this, but that is not Craig's approach). What can it mean to say God underwent a change at the end of which God was temporal? Craig's answer seems to be that there is timelessness before time's beginning, or rather, "before" time's beginning.

Craig endorses Padgett's distinction between "Measured Time" and "Ontological Time" (God's time). Unlike Padgett, he identifies the latter with Newton's absolute time. He defends a "neo-Lorentzian" interpretation of special relativity, according to which there is a privileged reference frame that is in principle undetectable due to the effective Lorentz invariance of the dynamical laws. In addition, he points to the cosmic time of some general relativistic spacetime models as a candidate for absolute time. Each of these claims is made in support of a strong prior commitment to the A-theory, shared with Padgett. However, each claim faces problems, and their connection is unclear, since the "neo-Lorentzian" approach to special relativity does not allow for as natural a development in the direction of general relativity as does the standard approach (see, e.g., Balashov & Janssen 2003, Wüthrich 2013).

Richard Swinburne's original view was a timeless one (Swinburne 1965), but he later switched to a version of divine temporality. Like Padgett, he thinks of God's time as metrically amorphous. However, he says that before creation God lives in this metrically amorphous time, and this same time then acquires a metric when God creates the world and institutes the laws of nature.

As we will see shortly, divine omniscience and God's knowledge of the future play a central role in arguments against timelessness. For this reason, a particular stance on divine foreknowledge deserves special mention here. In Open Theism, many facts about the future, in particular facts about human beings' future free decisions, are currently unknown to God (see, e.g., Rhoda 2007). Some Open Theists think the future is open in the sense that some propositions about the future lack a determinate truth-value. God is in time, finding out about the shape of the future as it unfolds. However, God is still omniscient; omniscience requires knowing all determinately true propositions.

Further defenses of divine temporality can be found in John Lucas (1973, 1989), Nicholas Wolterstorff (1975, 2000a, 2000b, 2001), William Hasker (1989, 2002), Dean Zimmerman 2002, Garrett DeWeese (2002, 2004), and Ryan Mullins (2016). As mentioned, the more straightforwardly temporal one's view of God, the less there is to say about the view itself (at least insofar as the view's claims about God's relationship to time are concerned), and the more there is to say about arguments for and against the view. So let us turn to the most important reasons that have been given for accepting divine temporality.

Perhaps the most widely discussed argument against the view that God is timeless is the argument about omniscience and tensed facts. The argument is of particular interest for our purposes because it has been a focal point for discussions about how the metaphysics of time, and the A versus B debate, impacts one's stance on God and time. I will discuss three different arguments, of which the first is the one that is most often discussed. Recall that it is only the A-theory that posits fundamental tensed facts (such as that it is 12:00). Does God know these tensed facts, if the A-theory is true? Well, God is omniscient, so presumably God knows them. This is the basis for Argument 1. (Different variations appear in Prior 1962; Craig 2000, 2001; DeWeese 2000, 2004; Hasker 2002; Kretzmann 1966; Padgett 1992, 2001; Wolterstorff 1975; Loftin 2015; Mullins 2016, ch. 4); the following variation also appears in Deng 2018b):

Argument 1
(1) God is omniscient.
(2) If God is omniscient, then God knows the fundamental temporal facts. So,
(3) God knows the fundamental temporal facts. (From (1), (2)) So,
(4) if there are fundamental tensed facts (i.e., the A-theory is true), then God knows them. (From (3))
(5) If God knows fundamental tensed facts, then what God knows changes.
(6) If what God knows changes, then God changes.
(7) If God changes, then God is temporal.

Therefore, if the A-theory is true, then God is temporal. (From (4), (5), (6), (7))

The intended upshot is that defenders of timelessness are "forced into" the B-theory. And since the B-theory is somewhat less popular within the philosophy of religion than it is elsewhere in philosophy, the argument is also often treated as an argument against divine timelessness. But some defenders of timelessness have indeed responded by embracing the B-theory (Helm 1988, 2001; Rogers 2000).

One can in principle respond by challenging any of the argument's premises (for different responses, see Wierenga 1989, 2002; Alston 1989; Ganssle 1993, 1995, 2002). But none are without difficulty. Katherin Rogers nicely brings out the urgency of the problem for a defender of divine timelessness contemplating giving up on God's omniscience:

> Were God outside of time in such a way that He sees all of time as if it were equally present, then He is missing one really crucial piece of information and that is what time it actually is right now. God may have numbered the hairs on your head, but He doesn't know whether you are presently dead or alive. A serious problem indeed! (Rogers 2006, 1)

The connection to the A versus B debate is a little more subtle than it is sometimes made out to be. Of course it is true that on the B-theory, the fundamental temporal facts are tenseless, so they do not change over time. A strictly parallel argument for the conclusion that on the B-theory, God is temporal too (if God is omniscient) would therefore not succeed. The equivalent of premise (5) would not be true. However, to leave matters there is to overstate the relevance of the metaphysics of time, and to understate the relevance of background assumptions about what a divine omniscient knower would be like. To see this, consider some variations on Argument 1 (Argument 2 and Argument 3 also appear in Deng 2018b):

Argument 2

(1′) God is omniscient.
(2′) If God is omniscient, then God knows what time it is. So,
(3′) God knows what time it is. (From (1′), (2′))
(4′) What time it is changes. So,
(5′) what God knows changes. (From (3′), (4′))
(6) If what God knows changes, then God changes.
(7) If God changes, then God is temporal.

Therefore, God is temporal. (From (5′), (6), (7))

Argument 2 already loosens the connection to the metaphysical issue somewhat because it is not couched in terminology taken straight from the A versus B debate. On reflection, we find that Argument 2 is indeed successful only if the A-theory is correct (as one might have expected from Argument 1); but this is not obvious at first sight, and thinking about Argument 2 is useful. Consider premises (3′) and (4′). We certainly want to affirm (3′). Is (4′) true, on the B-theory? In a sense, yes: there is, on the B-theory, a sense in which what time it is changes. That change is to be understood like other changes. For the B-theorist, change consists in variation over time. Something changes if at one time it has one property, and at another, later time it has a different, incompatible property. For the B-theorist, saying that a time is present is similar to saying a certain spatial location is here. Any time is present relative to itself, just like any spatial location is here relative to itself. So provided you think "It is now 12:00" or "12:00 is present" at 12:00, what you think is true. Similarly, a moment later, when you think "12:01 is present," provided you think it at 12:01, what you think is again true. There is no interesting sense in which time, on the B-theory, is ever "stuck." There is a succession of times, not just one time.

Here is a problem with running Argument 2 on the B-theory. On a standard B-theoretic account of tensed language, the content of each of these thoughts is tenseless. What one thinks, and what one knows, at each of these times, is something that one could know (and typically does know) at all times, namely for example, that 12:00 is simultaneous with 12:00. This tenseless content can also be truly believed via a tenseless sentence, namely "12:00 is simultaneous with 12:00." But only at 12:00 can it be truly believed via the tensed sentence "12:00 is present." How does this impact Argument 2? It suggests that according to the B-theory, it is not the case that knowing what time it is for a period of time involves gaining and losing pieces of knowledge. Therefore, it is presumably not the case, according to the B-theory, that what one knows changes. This in turn suggests that (5′) does not follow from (3′) and (4′).

Nonetheless, this is not quite the end of the story because, on this account of tensed language, what matters is not just what one believes at each time, but how one believes it. Believing something truly via a tensed sentence has a rather different cognitive significance than believing it via a tenseless sentence. This is also the case for other indexicals. Believing that John is making a mess via the representation "I am making a mess" has a different cognitive significance from believing it via "John is making a mess." (For more on these issues, see, e.g., Kaplan 1989; Perry 1979; Dyke 2003; Mozersky 2006.)

This suggests that we should consider the following argument.

Argument 3
(1′)　God is omniscient.
(2′)　If God is omniscient, then God knows what time it is. So,
(3′)　God knows what time it is. (From (1′), (2′))
(4″)　If S knows what time it is, then how S believes (what S believes) changes.
(5″)　How God believes (what God believes) changes. (From (3′), (4″))
(6″)　If how God believes changes, then God changes.
(7)　If God changes, then God is temporal.

Therefore, God is temporal. (From (5″), (6″), (7))

The point is that generally speaking, subjects in B-theoretic time need to vary their tensed beliefs ("It is noon," "It is 12:01") in order to keep track of their changing temporal perspectives.

One might object that God, unlike us, is able to act in a timely manner without tensed representations. We need tensed beliefs in order to keep track of our temporal perspective, and in order to act at the right times (e.g., get up and go to the meeting room at and only at noon, the starting time of the meeting). But God is in a different position. God can do all God ever does "all at once," from a standpoint equally outside all times.[10]

A couple of points are worth noting. The first is that Argument 3 does not mention God's actions, only God's knowledge. If the reason we were worried about an incompatibility between omniscience andtimelessness had to do with knowing what time it is, then that worry should not automatically disappear as soon as we embrace the B-theory. It is true that we humans need to know what time it is in order to act in a timely manner. But would not an omniscient being need to know what time it is, no matter what their mode of action may be?

Perhaps the intended answer is that God does know what time it is, but that for God, even in B-time, knowing what time it is just does not require any changes in how one believes (so that (4″) is not true of God). The question then becomes what knowing what time it is consists in, for God, on the B-theory. In any case, and this is the second point, whether this response is plausible will depend on rather more than whether time is A- or B-theoretic. This second point is a point of clarification as to the intended import of Argument 3. The argument's purpose is not to establish that on the B-theory, an omniscient God cannot be timeless. Rather, its purpose is to bring out that whether or not an omniscient God can be timeless does not really depend only on one's meta-physical allegiance (whether A or B). It depends on various background assumptions about what omniscience requires, including assumptions about which features of our temporal nature an omniscient being would share. On both A- and B-theoretic accounts of the world do we human beings often know what time it is. However, on only one of these, the A-theory, does this amount to knowing what the (current) fundamental (tensed) temporal facts are. On the B-theory, it amounts to something different – or, one might also say, to some-thing more. It amounts to not only knowing certain fundamental (tenseless) temporal facts, but also accessing these facts in a certain way. Perhaps this

---

[10] This is based on comments by Brian Leftow, but I do not claim that he would endorse the particular form of the objection I am addressing here.

something more is unimportant for an omniscient being, unlike knowing the fundamental temporal facts. But this is an additional substantial assumption that goes beyond which metaphysical model of time is correct.

Here is a different reason to worry about divine timelessness. Consider the relation of time to personhood. What does it take to be a person? Persons remember – they anticipate, reflect, deliberate, decide, and intend things. *Prima facie*, it is hard to see how a timeless being could do any of these things. How, then, could there be a timeless personal God?

There are things that friends of divine timelessness can say in reply. Perhaps being timeless is in fact a way of living the richest life a person can live. The divine person is *sui generis*, after all. Moreover, they might maintain that all it takes to be a person is the capability to do (at least some of) the things listed above (remembering, deliberating, anticipating, intending, etc.), and maybe a timeless personal God has the capability to do (at least some of) these things. It is just that instead of exercising these capabilities, God "lives his whole life in a single present of unimaginable intensity" (Leftow 2010, 278). A different response would be to maintain that timelessness does not prevent one from engaging in (all of) these activities.

Perhaps God's ways of remembering, deliberating, or intending, are just different from ours.

Finally, consider again our starting point: much of Western Scripture seems to be about God's relations to the created universe. God is said to know about the lives of God's creatures, and to respond to them in petitionary prayer. God perhaps also sustains the universe in existence at every moment. All of these are relations that God stands in to the universe. Arguably, a being cannot stand in causal and other relations to a temporal world without being temporal him- or herself.

5 Concluding Remarks

One of the byproducts of the recent move away from a traditional, "classical" view of God as outside of time and towards temporal views has been the potential for fruitful discussions about the aims and methods of theology and philosophy of religion. In a recent polemical study of divine timelessness, Ryan Mullins suggests that

> [T]heologians and philosophers should abandon the divine timeless research program because it is unworkable and devastating to Christian theology. Instead, they should devote their attention to developing models of divine temporality and the implications that it has for the rest of Christian theology.

> Divine timelessness has had a long run in Church history, but it is time to bury it and move on. (Mullins 2016)

Mullins critically analyzes a number of confusions that he thinks have permeated discussions about divine eternality. One of these (which he calls "Confusion No. 1") is a tendency on the part of some theologians to affirm that God is both temporal and timeless. As an example, he quotes Bruce Ware: "Amazingly, then, at creation God became both omnipresent and omnitemporal while remaining, in himself apart from creation, fully nonspatial and timelessly eternal" (Ware 2008, 89). Mullins responds that this is a flat contradiction and therefore unacceptable.

For someone who is following this discussion from outside of the theistic community (as I am), this is a fascinating encounter. Mullins's methodological stance is correct. It certainly will not do to bluntly assert a contradiction and leave it at that, or worse to revel in a lack of intelligibility. Contradictions are not acceptable when one is offering one's best description of what the world we live in is actually like. But at the same time, one has to wonder whether any theistic conception can completely eliminate contradiction while still being fit for its purpose. Perhaps there is in fact a *need* for mystery or even contradiction inherent in theistic religion. Such a need might be bound up with elements of religious practice. Of course, this is a substantial claim that requires an extended defense. But suffice it to say that it seems as if this conversation is only beginning, with difficulties yet to be faced on both sides.

The search for a philosophically and theologically adequate conception of God's relationship to time is ongoing, and it is an exciting time to join the search.

Bibliography

Alston, William P. (1984). Hartshorne and Aquinas: a via media. In J. Cobb and F. Gamwell, eds., *Existence and Actuality*. Chicago: University of Chicago Press.

(1989). Does God have beliefs? In Divine Nature and Human Language: Essays in Philosophical Theology. Ithaca and London: Cornell University Press, pp. 178–193.

Balashov, Yuri & Janssen, Michel. (2003). Presentism and relativity. *British Journal for the Philosophy of Science*, 54 (2): 327–346.

Baron, S., Cusbert, J., Farr, M., Kon, M. & Miller, K. (2015). Temporal experience, temporal passage, and the cognitive sciences. *Philosophy Compass* 10(8): 560–571.

Benovsky, Jiri. (2013). From experience to metaphysics: on experience-based intuitions and their role in metaphysics. *Noûs* 49(3): 684–697.

Boethius. (1973). *The Consolation of Philosophy*. Transl. V. E. Watts, London: Penguin Books, 1969; also transl. H. F. Stewart, E. K. Rand, and S. J. Tester, Loeb Classical Library. Cambridge: Harvard University Press.

Broad, C. D. (1938). *Examination of McTaggart's Philosophy*, Vol. II, Cambridge University Press.

Butterfield, Jeremy. (1984). Seeing the present. *Mind* 93 (370): 161–176.

Callender, Craig. (2017). *What Makes Time Special*. Oxford: Oxford University Press.

Craig, William L. (1999). The eternal present and Stump-Kretzmann eternity. *American Catholic Philosophical Quarterly* 73: 521–536.

(2000). Timelessness and omnitemporality. *Philosophia Christi*, Series 2, (2/1): 29–33.

(2001). *Time and Eternity: Exploring God's Relationship to Time*. Wheaton IL: Crossway Books.

(2009). Divine eternity. In M. C. Rea and T. P. Flint, eds., *The Oxford Handbook of Philosophical Theology*. Oxford: Oxford University Press.

Dainton, Barry. (2008). The experience of time and change. *Philosophy Compass* 3/4: 619–638.

Deng, Natalja. (2013a). Fine's McTaggart, temporal passage, and the A versus B debate. *Ratio* 26(1): 19–34.

(2013b). On explaining why time seems to pass. *Southern Journal of Philosophy* 51(3): 367–382.

(2015). On whether B-theoretic atheists should fear death. *Philosophia* 43 (4): 1011–1021.

(2018a). What is temporal ontology? *Philosophical Studies*, 175/3: 793–807.

(2018b). Eternity in Christian thought. The Stanford Encyclopedia of Philosophy (Summer 2018 Edition), Edward N. Zalta (ed.), https://plato.stanford.edu/archives/sum2018/entries/eternity/.

(forthcoming). Time, metaphysics of. The Routledge Encyclopedia of Philosophy, www.rep.routledge.com/articles/thematic/time-metaphysics-of/v-1.

DeWeese, Garrett J. (2000). Timeless God, timeless time. *Philosophia Christi* 2/1: 53–59 l.

(2002). Atemporal, sempiternal or omnitemporal: God's temporal mode of being. In Ganssle and Woodruff 2002, pp. 49–61.

(2004). *God and the Nature of Time*, Aldershot, Hants.: Ashgate.

Dorato, Mauro. (2015). Presentism and the experience of time. *Topic* 34(1): 265–275.

Dummett, Michael. (1960). A defense of McTaggart's proof of the unreality of time. *Philosophical Review* 69 (4): 497–504.

Dyke, Heather. (2003). Tensed meaning: a tenseless account. *Journal of Philosophical Research* 27: 67–83.

Earman, John. (2008). Reassessing the prospects for a growing block model of the universe. *International Studies in the Philosophy of Science* 22 (2): 135–164.

Einstein, Albert & Besso, Michele. (1972). *Correspondance, 1903–1955*. Transl. by Pierre Speziali. Paris: Hermann.

Fales, Evan M. (1997). Divine intervention. *Faith and Philosophy* 14 (2): 170–194.

Falk, Arthur. (2003). Time plus the whoosh and whiz. In Aleksandar Jokic and Quentin Smith (eds.), *Time, Tense and Reference*. Cambridge, MA: Massachusetts Institute of Technology Press, pp. 211–250.

Fine, Kit. (2006). The reality of tense. *Synthese* 150 (3): 399–414.

Fitzgerald, Paul. (1985). Stump and Kretzmann on time and eternity. *The Journal of Philosophy* 82: 260 269.

Frischhut, Akiko. (2013). What experience cannot teach us about time. *Topoi* 1: 1–13.

Ganssle, Gregory E. (1993). Atemporality and the mode of divine knowledge. *International Journal for the Philosophy of Religion*, 34: 171–180.

(1995). Leftow on direct awareness and atemporality. *Sophia* 34: 30–3.

(2001). *God and Time: Four Views*. Downers Grove, IL: Inter Varsity Press.

(2002). Direct awareness and God's experience of a temporal now. In Ganssle and Woodruff 2002, pp. 165–181.

Ganssle, Gregory E. & Woodruff, David M. eds. (2002). *God and Time: Essays on the Divine Nature*, Oxford: Oxford University Press.

Grünbaum, Adolf. (1967). The status of temporal becoming. *Annals of the New York Academy of Sciences* 138: 374–395.

Hartshorne, Charles. (1947). *The Divine Relativity*. New Haven: Yale University Press.

Hasker, William, (1989). *God, Time, and Knowledge*. Ithaca, NY: Cornell University Press

(2002). The absence of a timeless God. In Ganssle and Woodruff 2002, pp. 182–206.

Helm, Paul. (1988). *Eternal God*. Oxford: Clarendon Press.

(2001). Divine timeless eternity. In Ganssle 2001, pp. 28–60.

Hoerl, Christoph. (2014a). Do we (seem to) perceive passage? *Philosophical Explorations* 17(2): 188–202.

(2014b). Time and the domain of consciousness. *Annals of the New York Academy of Sciences* 1326: 90–96.

Horwich, Paul. (1987). *Asymmetries in Time: Problems in the Philosophy of Science*. Cambridge, MA: Massachusetts Institute of Technology Press.

Inman, R. (2016). Omnipresence and the location of the immaterial. In J. Kvanvig (ed.) *Oxford Studies in Philosophy of Religion* Vol. 7, Oxford: Oxford University Press.

Ismael, Jenann. (2011). Temporal experience. In C. Callender (ed.), *The Oxford Handbook of Philosophy of Time*. Oxford: Oxford University Press.

James, William. (1890). *The Principles of Psychology*. New York: Henry Holt.

Kaplan, D. (1989). Demonstratives. In Almog, Perry, and Wettstein (eds.) *Themes From Kaplan*. Oxford: Oxford University Press, 481–563.

Kenny, Anthony. (1979). *The God of the Philosophers*. Oxford: Clarendon Press.

Kretzmann, Norman. (1966). Omniscience and immutability. *The Journal of Philosophy* 63: 409–421.

Leftow, Brian. (1991). *Time and Eternity*. Ithaca: Cornell University Press.

(2005). Eternity and immutability. In William Mann, ed., *The Blackwell Guide to the Philosophy of Religion*. Oxford and New York:Blackwell.

(2010). Eternity. In Charles Taliaferro, Paul Draper, Philip L. Quinn, eds., *A Companion to Philosophy of Religion*, 2nd ed. Oxford and New York: Blackwell.

(2016). Immutability. The Stanford Encyclopedia of Philosophy (Winter 2016 Edition), Edward N. Zalta (ed.), URL = <https://plato.stanford.edu /archives/win2016/entries/immutability/>

Lewis, David. (1986). *On the Plurality of Worlds*. Oxford: Blackwell Publishing.

Lewis, Delmas. (1984). Eternity again: a reply to Stump and Kretzmann. *International Journal for Philosophy of Religion* 15: 73–79.

Le Poidevin, R. (2007). *The Images of Time: An Essay on Temporal Representation*. Oxford: Oxford University Press.

Loftin, R. Keith. (2015). On the metaphysics of time and divine eternality. *Philosophia Christi* 17/1: 177–187.

Lucas, John R. (1973). *A Treatise on Time and Space*. London: William Clowes and Sons Limited.

(1989). *The Future: An Essay on God, Temporality and Truth*. Cambridge: Basil Blackwell Inc.

Maimonides, Moses. *The Guide of the Perplexed*. Transl. with an introduction by Shlomo Pines, with an introductory essay by Leo Strauss, Chicago: The University of Chicago Press, 1963.

Mawson, T. J. (2008). Divine eternity. *International Journal for Philosophy of Religion*, 64(1): 35–50.

McTaggart, John M. E. (1908). The unreality of time. *Mind* 17: 456–473.

Mellor, D. Hugh. (1998). *Real Time II*. London: Routledge.

(2001). The time of our lives. *Royal Institute of Philosophy Supplement* 48: 45–59.

Mozersky, M. Joshua. (2006). A tenseless account of the presence of experience. *Philosophical Studies* 129: 441–476.

Mullins, Ryan T. (2014). Doing hard time: Is God the prisoner of the oldest dimension? *Journal of Analytic Theology* 2: 160–185.

(2016). *The End of the Timeless God, Oxford Studies in Analytic Theology*. Oxford: Oxford University Press.

Nelson, Herbert J. (1987). Time(s), eternity, and duration. *International Journal for Philosophy of Religion* 22, No. 1/2: 3–19.

Ney, Alyssa. (2014). *Metaphysics: An Introduction*. Routledge.

Norton, J. D. (2010). Time really passes. *Humana Mente: Journal of Philosophical Studies* 13: 23–34.

Oppy, Graham. (1998). Some Emendations to Leftow's Arguments about Time and Eternity, on the Secular Web https://infidels.org/library/modern/gra ham_oppy/leftow.html; a revised version is incorporated into Oppy 2014.

(2014). *Describing Gods: An Investigation of Divine Attributes*. Cambridge: Cambridge University Press.

Padgett, Alan G. (1992). *God, Eternity and the Nature of Time*. London: Macmillan.

(2001). Eternity as Relative Timelessness, in Ganssle 2001, pp. 92–110.

Pasnau, R. (2011). On existing all at once. In Tapp, Christian and Runggaldier, Edmund, eds. *God, Eternity, and Time*, Aldershot: Ashgate Press, pp. 11–28.

Paul, Laurie A. (2010). Temporal experience. *The Journal of Philosophy* CVII: 333–59.

Perry, John. (1979). The problem of the essential indexical. *Nous* 13: 3–21.

Phillips, Ian. (2010). Perceiving temporal properties. *European Journal of Philosophy* 18 (2): 176–202

(2017). *The Routledge Handbook of Philosophy of Temporal Experience*. New York: Routledge.

Pike, Nelson C. (1970). *God and Timelessness*. New York: Schocken.

(1965). Divine omniscience and voluntary action. *The Philosophical Review*, 74(1): 27–46.

Pooley, Oliver. (2013). Relativity, the open future, and the passage of time. *Proceedings of the Aristotelian Society* 113(3pt3), pp. 321–363.

Prior, A. N. (1962). The formalities of omniscience. *Philosophy* 37: 114–129.

Prosser, Simon. (2016). *Experiencing Time*. Oxford: Oxford University Press.

Rea, Michael C. & Murray, Michael J. (2008). *An Introduction to the Philosophy of Religion, Cambridge Introductions to Philosophy*. Cambridge: Cambridge University Press.

Rhoda, Alan. (2007). The philosophical case for open theism. *Philosophia* 35: 301–11.

Rogers, Katherin A. (1994). Eternity has no duration. *Religious Studies* 30: 1–16.

(2000). *Perfect Being Theology*. Edinburgh: Edinburgh University Press.

(2006). Anselm on eternity as the fifth dimension. *The Saint Anselm Journal* 3.2: 1–8.

(2007). Anselmian eternalism: the presence of a timeless God. *Faith and Philosophy* 24: 3–27.

Sider, Theodore. (1996). All the world's a stage. *Australasian Journal of Philosophy*, 74: 433–453

(2001). *Four-Dimensionalism: An Ontology of Persistence and Time*. Oxford: Clarendon Press.

Skow, Bradford. (2009). Relativity and the moving spotlight. *Journal of Philosophy*, 106: 666–678.

(2015). *Objective Becoming*. Oxford: Oxford University Press.

Stump, Eleonore & Kretzmann, Norman. (1981). Eternity. *Journal of Philosophy* 78(8): 429–458.

(1987). Atemporal duration: a reply to Fitzgerald. *Journal of Philosophy* 84 (4): 214–219.

(1992). Eternity, awareness, and action. *Faith and Philosophy* 9 (4): 463–482.

Swinburne, Richard. (1965). The timelessness of God. *Church Quarterly Review*, 116: 323–337.

(1977). *The Coherence of Theism*. Oxford: Clarendon Press.

(1993). God and time. In Eleonore Stump, ed., *Reasoned Faith*. Ithaca: Cornell University Press, p. 204.

(1994). *The Christian God*. Oxford: Clarendon Press.

Tallant, Jonathan. (2012). (Existence) presentism and the A-theory. *Analysis* 72 (4): 673–681.

(2013). Recent work: time. *Analysis* 73 (2): 369–379.

Tooley, Michael. (1997). *Time, Tense and Causation*. Oxford: Clarendon Press.

Ware, Bruce. (2008). A modified Calvinist doctrine of God. In Bruce Ware, ed., *Perspectives on the Doctrine of God: 4 Views*. Nashville, TN: B and H Publishing.

Wierenga, Edward R. (1989). *The Nature of God: An Inquiry into Divine Attributes*. Ithaca: Cornell University Press.

(2002). Timelessness out of Mind, in Ganssle and Woodruff 2002, pp. 153–164.

Wolterstorff, Nicholas. (1975). God everlasting. In Clifton Orlebeke and Lewis Smedes, eds., *God and the Good: Essays in Honor of Henry Stob*. Grand Rapids, MI: Eerdmans, pp. 181–203.

(2000a). God and time. *Philosophia Christi* 2: 5–10.

(2000b). God is "everlasting," not "eternal". In Brian Davies, ed., *Philosophy of Religion: A Guide and Anthology*. New York: Oxford University Press.

(2001). Unqualified divine temporality, in Ganssle 2001, pp. 187–213.

Wüthrich, Christian. (2013). The fate of presentism in modern physics. In Roberto Ciunti, Kristie Miller, and Giuliano Torrengo, eds., *New Papers on the Present, Focus on Presentism*. Munich: Philosophia Verlag.

Wüthrich, Christian and Callender, Craig. (2017). What becomes of a causal set? *British Journal for the Philosophy of Science* 68 (3): 907–925.

Yates, John C. (1990). *The Timelessness of God*. Lanham: University Press of America.

Zagzebski, Linda. (1991). *The Dilemma of Freedom and Foreknowledge*. New York: Oxford University Press.

Zimmerman, Dean. (2002). God inside time and before creation, in Ganssle and Woodruff 2002, pp. 75–94.

(2005). The A-theory of time, the B-theory of time, and "taking tense seriously." *Dialectica* 59: 401–57.

(2011). Presentism and the space-time manifold. In C. Callender, ed., *The Oxford Handbook of Philosophy of Time*, Oxford: Oxford University Press, pp. 163–244.

Cambridge Elements ⹀

Philosophy of Religion

Yujin Nagasawa

University of Birmingham

Yujin Nagasawa is Professor of Philosophy and Co-Director of the John Hick Centre for Philosophy of Religion at the University of Birmingham. He is currently President of the British Society for the Philosophy of Religion. He is a member of the Editorial Board of *Religious Studies*, the *International Journal for Philosophy of Religion and Philosophy Compass.*

About the Series

This Cambridge Elements series provides concise and structured introductions to all the central topics in the philosophy of religion. It offers balanced, comprehensive coverage of multiple perspectives in the philosophy of religion. Contributors to the series are cutting-edge researchers who approach central issues in the philosophy of religion. Each provides a reliable resource for academic readers and develops new ideas and arguments from a unique viewpoint.

Cambridge Elements ⹀

Philosophy of Religion

Printed in the United States
By Bookmasters